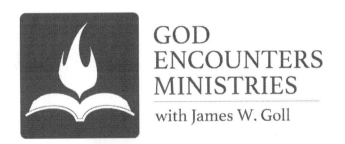

GOD
ENCOUNTERS
MINISTRIES

with James W. Goll

Published by
God Encounters Ministries
PO Box 1653
Franklin, TN 37065
www.godencounters.com

Copyright © 2016 James W. Goll
All rights reserved

Unless otherwise indicated, scripture is taken from the
New American Standard Bible®,
Copyright © 1960, 1962, 1963, 1968, 1971, 1972, 1973,
1975, 1977, 1995 by The Lockman Foundation
Used by permission. (www.Lockman.org)

As noted, scripture taken from the HOLY BIBLE, NEW INTERNATIONAL VERSION® (NIV)
Copyright © 1973, 1978, 1984 International Bible Society.
Used by permission of Zondervan. All rights reserved.

Scripture quotations marked (AMP) are taken from the Amplified Bible,
Copyright © 1954, 1958, 1962, 1964, 1965, 1987 by The Lockman Foundation.
Used by permission.

As noted, scripture taken from the King James Version (KJV)
The KJV is public domain in the United States.

All scripture is indicated by italics.

What Others Are Saying

I have known this man for many years and his life with God has impacted mine. James moves in a high realm of revelation but writes in a very down-to-earth and practical way about hearing God's voice. This foundational study guide will change your life and equip you to help others in their walk with God.

Dr. Ché Ahn
Author, *How to Pray for Healing* and *Hosting the Holy Spirit*
Founder of H Rock Church and Harvest International Ministries
Pasadena, California

Some years ago, when we were looking for a prophetic voice to bring to the Nashville, TN area to help us learn to listen for God, we called James Goll. We were not disappointed with his easy-to-apply guidelines for following hard after the voice of God. *Hearing and Obeying God's Voice* is exactly what the title indicates – an easy-to-read, easy-to-apply guide to listening to God and discerning how God is speaking to you. I find that it also has good reminders for those of us who have been listening for a while.

Dr. Don Finto
Founder of Caleb Company
Author, *Your People Shall Be My People*

Imagine if you heard God's voice with confident clarity. You would never again make a bad decision, choose a wrong relationship or question your next move. Don't spend another day confused about God's voice or guidance, or traipse from conference to conference in hopes of a hearing impartation! James Goll's *Hearing and Obeying God's Voice Study Guide* is like a graduate level course in recognizing God's voice, but the only prerequisite you need is childlike faith!

Laura Harris Smith, C.N.C.,
Co-Pastor of East Gate Creative Christian Fellowship
Author of *Seeing the Voice of God* and *The 30-Day Faith Detox*

James Goll has lived life for many years filled with the experience of hearing God's voice. All of us have much we can learn from him and this study guide and with its corresponding book gives all of us tips from one who knows.

John Arnott
Founding Leader, Catch the Fire
Toronto, Ontario, Canada

After observing James Goll in ministry, it would be extremely easy to conclude that he has reached an unattainable dimension of clarity in hearing from God, and that he is a one-of-a-kind modern-day Elijah. James decided not to let the Body of Christ off the hook so easily. This study guide and the accompanying book have been written with every believer in mind. It demystifies the process of hearing from God and invites the reader into a deeper relationship with the Lord. *Hearing and Obeying God's Voice* covers theological and devotional approaches to hearing from God in a disarmingly simple but profound perspective. Get ready for a life-changing experience.

Harry R. Jackson, Jr.
Senior Pastor, Hope Christian Church
Washington, D.C.

If you have ever longed to hear God in a clearer way, *Hearing and Obeying God's Voice* is for you. James Goll has long had an intimate relationship with God and knows how to communicate well what God has taught him. This study guide and book guide you in practical and biblical ways in learning how to listen more closely. If you are willing, you can move from a hard-to-receive (HTR) position to one he calls ETR – easy-to-receive. Fresh insights he shares from recent experiences will make us desire to listen more closely for the voice of the Holy Spirit with attentive and expectant hearts. Thanks, James, for additional training resources!

Quin Sherrer
Author, *Women's Guide to Spiritual Warfare* and many other titles

Dedication

With an overflowing heart of thanksgiving, I wish to dedicate this *Hearing and Obeying God's Voice Study Guide*, to two of my mentors in these ways of God. The Holy Spirit brought these two gifted men into my life, and they have made a dramatic impact on my calling and destiny.

Years ago, Mahesh Chavda, presently of All Nations Church in Fort Mills, South Carolina, taught me some of his best-kept secrets about hearing God. I watched, I listened and I learned from a man who spent time with God. I have had the honor of walking with Mahesh since the early days of our mutual ministries. May the Lord reward you, Mahesh.

I also wish to acknowledge and give honor to my "prophetic-seer papa", the late Bob Jones. This dear gifted man of God took me under his wing in the early years of the prophetic movement in Kansas City. Bob Jones was one of the greatest "seer of seers" in modern Christianity. Wow. I miss you Bob! I still carry your impartations and promise to pass them on to the next generation of young eagles.

Thank you Lord for Your gifts to me in Mahesh Chavda and Bob Jones.

With Gratitude,

Dr. James W. Goll

Acknowledgments

Deep gratitude goes to the past and present staff at God Encounters Ministries for their support in every project I undertake. This *Hearing and Obeying God's Voice Study Guide* is a labor of love that contains the fingerprints of so many wonderful people!

I want to thank my personal Prayer Shield, chaired by Kay Durham and with the assistance of many others prayerful believers who have faithfully held up my hands. Special thanks go to Jeffrey Thompson, my Executive Director and Don Clark, my IT Director. They and others have served me with excellence over the years.

I also wish to thank my friend, Quin Sherrer, who opened the door for the initial publishing of the original manuscript with Servant / Vine Publications. Later this became a part of The Beginners Guide series that was adopted into the Regal Books family. There it went through two revisions as well. Kathy Deering became my consistent writing and editing assistant through all these transitions. Kathy has been a gift from God to my life and thus yours.

Eventually, the book was re-envisioned and reshaped by my long time publishing friends at Baker / Chosen Books. What started out as my shortest book for beginners has now been flipped into a marvelous book full of scriptures, stories and practical tools to help anyone at any point in their developmental journey to help them cultivate a closer relationship with God. And of course, along with the book came this complementary *Hearing and Obeying God's Voice Study Guide*.

Now an entire curriculum kit including this *Hearing and Obeying God's Voice Study Guide*, the *Hearing God's Voice Today* Book, and 12 Message Class Set are available as well as well. This set of materials has taken years to develop – so it is a joy to now pass it on to you!

And yes, God still speaks today. Are you listening?

Ever Listening,

Dr. James W. Goll

Table of Contents

Foreword by Mickey Robinson 11

Preface by James W. Goll 13

Lesson One: As It Was in the Beginning 15

Lesson Two: The Holy Spirit at Work Today 21

Lesson Three: The Sound of Many Rushing Waters 27

Lesson Four: Walking in Our Kingdom Birthright 35

Lesson Five: Built Upon the Rock 41

Lesson Six: Ten Practical, Personal Tools 49

Lesson Seven: Walking in Community 55

Lesson Eight: Hearing with Discernment 61

Lesson Nine: He Will Guide You! 69

Lesson Ten: Listening, Waiting and Watching 75

Lesson Eleven: Properly Responding to God's Voice 81

Lesson Twelve: At the End of the Day 89

Reflection Question Answers 97

End Notes 99

Foreword
by Mickey Robinson

Writing the foreword to this study guide is both an honor and a challenge because of my personal experience and very close relationship with the author. My wife Barbara and I met James and his wife and family at least 25 years ago. Not only have we worked together intensely, our families have been very close personally. It is an honor because this study guide represents some of the most important foundational tools in being a true follower/disciple of Jesus Christ the Messiah. It is a challenge because I wish I wrote this manual and will have to resist the temptation not to preach in writing this foreword!

Hearing the voice of God is NOT a specialty gift, an optional characteristic, or a designated attribute to a certain denomination of believers. It is a defining, actively ongoing dynamic in the personal relationship with the Lord of the universe. It is a lifelong journey learning to hear, interpret, discern, and most importantly, to simply obey the Voice of the Shepherd. *"My sheep hear My voice, and I know them, and they follow Me."* John 10:27. This colossal verse of Scripture precedes the promise of eternal life and the vigilance of the Lord being a good shepherd that will not allow anyone to snatch His followers out of His hand.

James is a masterful teacher on this essential aspect of communion with God. He is an authentic teacher because he actually lives this way: simply listening, discerning, and obeying what he hears the Lord saying.

Jesus strongly addressed these truths to his disciples in the parable of the sower in Mark, 4. The first word He said at this encounter was *"Listen"* or in the King James version, *"Hearken."* He was sharing before a large crowd of people so vast that He had to get in a boat to create space between Him and the multitude. After He finished the parable He said, *"He who has ears to hear, let him hear!"*

Then they all left, except those who were truly following Him. Once when they were alone with him, He told them, *"to you it has been given to know the mystery of the kingdom of God; but to those who are outside, all things come in parables..."* Jesus then said to them, "Do you not understand this parable? How then will you understand all the parables?" In other words, He was saying, "If you don't get this one you won't get any of them." It is clear to me that this parable is about the ability to perceive the revelation of the word of God or "Hearing the Voice of God."

These 12 lessons present concise tools on how each of us can fine-tune our hearing and applying the guidance of the Holy Spirit. Each of us must personally know how to implement spiritual things into practical living. Jesus sums up his Sermon on the Mount discourse (Matthew 5-7) saying, *"Therefore, whoever HEARS these sayings of mine and does them, I will liken him to a wise man who built his house on the rock..."* He continues to elaborate that when a storm comes the house will STAND and storms do come.

It is never too late to seek to live by the Word of the Lord both written and spoken. He is merciful in spite of our well-meaning but failed attempts to obey Him in our own strength. He wants us to desire to seek His voice, and as we do He is ready to grant us the grace to obey Him.

As one wise father of the faith said recently, "God doesn't hide things from us, He hides things for us." In your hand is a refined, practical manual of how you can hear His Voice and walk in His grace. This is not something James Goll learned at a school or from somebody else. It is more than four decades of full-time ministry and the personal pilgrimage of a modern-day mystic who is one of my very closest companions.

In closing, Jeremiah 33:3 says, *"Call to Me, and I will answer you, and show you great and mighty things, which you do not know."* As you put into practice the principles laid out in this study guide, I believe these words will come to pass for you.

Great job, James! This manual is for everyone.

With Honor,

Mickey Robinson,
Co-Founder of Prophetic Destiny International
International Speaker, Author and a Real Friend

Preface
by James W. Goll

God still speaks today! Are you listening? What are you hearing? Is your faith growing as a result of your interpersonal communion with God? While we agree that the canon of scripture is closed, we also believe that Jesus Christ is the same, yesterday, today and forever (Hebrews 13:8). What He did before He continues to do. God has spoken, God speaks and God's promises to continue to speak to us.

One of the on-going activities of the Holy Spirit is listening and then communicating. The Holy Spirit speaks to us what He hears. *"But when He, the Spirit of truth, comes, He will guide you into all the truth; for He will not speak on His own initiative, but whatever He hears, He will speak; and He will disclose to you what is to come."* (John 16:13)

One of the most overlooked ministries of the Holy Spirit is that of listening. He listens before He speaks. We need to take some lessons from the nature and character of the Holy Spirit!

The Ever Proceeding Word

Let's take a quick look at this Old Testament verse quoted by Jesus in the New Testament. It is essential to grasp the first half of the verse in order to receive the promise stated in the second half.

> *"He humbled you and let you be hungry, and fed you with manna which you did not know, nor did your fathers know, that He might make you understand that man does not live by bread alone, but man lives by everything that proceeds out of the mouth of the LORD."*
> (Deuteronomy 8:3)

Look at these progressive steps: first comes humility; second comes hunger; third is being fed fresh manna; and finally, you are made to understand. Spiritual hunger seems to be paramount. Are you hungry for God and His ever-proceeding word? It is the hungry that are fed things, which they formerly knew nothing about. There are always new things to learn from God. There are always new things in God's heart He wants to share with His people.

Satan himself confronted Jesus and He overcame the devil by declaring the written word of God. Matthew 4:4 states, *"But He [Jesus] answered and said, "It is written, 'Man shall not live on bread alone, but on every word that proceeds out of the mouth of God.'"*

This is why I composed this practical study guide with 12 lessons to accompany my book, *Hearing God's Voice Today*. I want to give you some vintage materials and personal tips that have been given to me. Oh how I love His voice! How about you?

Blessings to You in Christ Jesus!

Dr. James W. Goll

Lesson One:
As It Was in the Beginning

"My sheep hear My voice, and I know them, and they follow Me."
John 10:27

"Behold, I stand at the door and knock; if anyone hears My voice and opens the door, I will come in to him and will dine with him, and he with Me."
Revelation 3:20

I. IT TAKES TWO TO COMMUNICATE

A. Does God Really Speak Today?

Will He speak personally to me? If I listen, will He speak in such a manner that even I can understand? As we go on this journey together in this study guide, we are going to discover that the answer is YES! And, believe it or not, God Himself wants all of us to hear what He is saying–more than any of us do! But we must remember that all communication requires two–not just one.

Because God is our Creator, the One who formed us, we have an inner longing to hear and know the voice of our Creator. The opening chapter to my book *Hearing God's Voice Today* says: "He didn't make us to be mechanical robots that just march around doing preordained things. Our Father God created us to have fellowship with Him. It is our birthright to have an actual relationship with our God."[1] And that relationship requires communication.

B. Communication with God Goes Two Ways

1. Talking to Him
2. Listening to Him When He talks to Us

To have good communication, we must learn how and when to speak up and how and when to push the pause button in order to listen. Fellowship is not a one-way road. It takes two! Both parties–in one another's presence–sharing attentively in back and forth dialogue together. "Available" is God's middle name. He is just aching to spend time each of us. He yearns to hear from us. He wants us to know how attentive He is.

C. What Others Have to Say

1. Mark Virkler, author and leader of Christian Leadership University states, "The voice of God, I've discovered, is Spirit-to-spirit communication, the Holy Spirit speaking directly to my spirit."[2]
2. Dutch Sheets, author, intercessor and statesman has stated, "What topic could possibly deserve more of our attention than listening to God? When the source of all life and wisdom speaks, those who would be wise listen. The foolish either don't care to or don't learn how. The fruit of both is the same: destructive ignorance."[3]

II. HOW IT BEGAN WITH ME

A. Influences in My Early Years
Jesus was always right there with me as my close friend.

B. College Years and the Collision with the Jesus People
My quest led me into divine collision with a group of people with whom I had little in common–the Jesus People. I eventually got filled with the Holy Spirit and released into His gifts. I was absolutely transformed.

C. Suddenly Life Was Different
I began to experience Knowings, Hunches, Burdens, Desires, Impressions–I had been given a Hearing Aid!

III. A DESIRE FOR DISCERNMENT

A. A Revelation from John 10:27 & Revelation 3:20
The place to begin is always the Word of God!

B. My Encounter at the Episcopal Church
I knelt in prayer and simply said, "Lord, I ask that You enroll me in Your School of the Spirit. Teach me not only how to hear, but also how to discern Your voice from the voice of the stranger and all the other voices that contend for my attention. Please do this so that I can truly follow You."

C. The Book of Godly Desires
What is being written in your book?

IV. LESSONS FROM THE ORIGINAL COUPLE

A. A Glance at the Book of Beginnings
A good starting place in our personal School of the Spirit is the lesson we can learn from the original couple, Adam and Eve, as recorded in Genesis 3. After they tasted the forbidden fruit, God came looking for fellowship with Adam and Eve–to walk and talk with them (as He does with you and me).

B. Here's the Good News
God is searching for us. He is drawing near–whether we want Him to or not!

V. LESSONS FROM THE PIONEERS OF FAITH
Many pilgrims of the faith have walked the path of communicating with God before us. We can look to them and learn both from their failures and their successes.

A. A Glance into the Life of Abraham
This man heard impossible promises from God, things that would require God's presence for their fulfillment. Abraham had to feel rather desperate and dependent, don't you think? God required much of Abraham, stepping in only when His intervention was needed!

B. The Big Test Came!
God spoke to Abraham to take his son and offer him as a sacrifice on Mount Moriah. (See Genesis 22:1-2.) What a test! But Abraham obeyed, and what an outcome!

C. The Grace of Yielding
We must each learn to walk as pilgrims of faith holding onto nothing and giving all to Him in every season.

D. The Friend of God
Abraham was called the friend of God (see 2 Chronicles 20:7). I, too, want to be a friend of God. In fact, that is what I think hearing God's voice is all about.

VI. WE EACH HAVE A DESPERATE NEED

A. Joining with the Cry of Others
Abraham, Moses, Mary and Paul were only ordinary people like us. Every person ever created has a need and a deep longing to hear their Creator's voice. Each person can talk to God, and they can hear Him, too. Each person is created with the need to be continuously dependent on His voice.

B. How Desperate Are You?
I think of the words of an old hymn: "I need Thee, oh, I need Thee; every hour I need Thee."[4]

VII. YOU CAN START NOW! CLOSING INVITATIONAL PRAYER

Dear Lord, I want to hear Your voice and learn Your ways. Be my teacher and guide. Enroll me in the School of the Spirit, and teach me to hear Your voice. Write down my name! I want to know You, to be a disciple of Christ Jesus, and to have sweet communion with You. I want to hear You, have more faith, and obey what You tell me. Help, Lord, for Your servant wants to listen. Amen.

Reflection Questions
Lesson One: As It Was in the Beginning

Answers to these questions can be found in the back of the study guide.

Fill in the Blank

1. List two ways communication with God takes place:

    a. _____

    b. _____

2. _____ with God is not a one-way road. It takes two!

3. When the source of all life and wisdom speaks, those who would be wise are those who _____.

Multiple Choice — Choose the best answer from the list below:

    A. Dedication   C. Blessing

    B. Discernment   D. Fellowship

4. When you have a desire for _____, or to know things you cannot know on your own, the best place to begin is the Word of God.

5. In the book of Genesis, Chapter 3, we find an interaction that the original couple, Adam and Eve, had with God called _____.

Continued on the next page.

True or False

6. God is drawing near to us, whether we want Him to or not. _____

7. God spoke to Abraham to offer his son on Mount Sinai. _____

8. Abraham was called an obedient servant of God. _____

Scripture Memorization

9. Write out 2 Chronicles 20:7 and memorize it.

Lesson Two:
The Holy Spirit at Work Today

"But I tell you the truth, it is to your advantage that I go away; for if I do not go away, the Helper will not come to you; but if I go, I will send Him to you."
John 16:7

"However, when He, the Spirit of truth, has come, He will guide you into all truth; for He will not speak on His own authority, but whatever He hears He will speak; and He will tell you things to come."
John 16:13 NKJV

"When the Helper comes, whom I will send to you from the Father, that is the Spirit of truth who proceeds from the Father, He will testify about Me."
John 15:26

Our Papa God has many gifts to give to us. The biggest gift of all, of course, is His Son, Jesus–the beloved Son, who, through the work of the cross, purchased for us our salvation. Our heavenly Father gave us His very heart in that one gift. Jesus is the greatest gift of all.

Additionally, Father and Son have sent their best by giving each disciple one very special gift, a gift that keeps giving more gifts. What could that be? He's our Comforter, our Guide, the One called to be alongside us and to help–the Holy Spirit. And the Holy Spirit is at work today in each of our lives!

I. THE THIRD PERSON OF THE GODHEAD

A. Who Is the "Holy Ghost"?
The Apostles' Creed, that I learned to recite in church every Sunday, stated so simply: "I believe in the Holy Ghost." That was it. So I was in the dark concerning the precious Third Person of the Godhead. I didn't understand who He was.

B. Today–He Is So Much More!
The Holy Spirit indeed is my Friend, Partner, Guide and my Co-conspirator. He wants to be yours, as well.

C. Insights from Others

1. From Authors Quin Sherrer and Ruthanne Garlock
"What an extraordinary gift the Father bestowed upon his children when he sent the Holy Spirit to be our helper! Is it any wonder that Satan tries to minimize the significance of the gift and divide and confuse the body of Christ concerning it?"[5]

2. From Evangelist David Wilkerson, founder of Teen Challenge
"Give much quality time to communion with the Holy Spirit. He will not speak to anyone who is in a hurry. All of God's Word is about waiting on Him! Wait patiently. Seek the Lord and minister praises to Him. Take authority over every other voice that whispers thoughts to you. Believe that the Spirit is greater than these, and that He will not let you be deceived or blind. Be willing to set your heart on Him."[6]

II. THE TUTOR OF GOD'S PERSONAL TOUCH

A. Definitions of the Word Tutor
Let's glance at how the word tutor is described in the dictionary:

1. **tutor** *n*: a person charged with the instruction and guidance of another as a private teacher
2. **tutor** *vt* 1: to have guardianship, tutelage, or care of 2: to teach or guide usually individually in a special subject or for a particular purpose: COACH ~ *vi* 1: to do the work of a tutor 2: to receive instruction especially privately[7]

B. What Person Has Influenced Your Life the Most?
Often people answer with the name of a special schoolteacher or coach they had when growing up. I know what my answer is. Besides Jesus Himself, the Holy Spirit has made more impact on my life than any person. Why? He is always personal and full of grace and truth!

III. THE TEACHER OF MANY CLASSES
The authors of scripture describe the amazing variety of classes offered in God's "School of the Spirit." Over the past 2,000 years, many Christians just like you and I have taken these classes and put their knowledge into action. Do you want to take advantage of God's best for you? Below are just a few of the possible courses.

A. Holiness 101: Read John 16:8-11
What are you going to learn in this class? How will that impact your life or the lives of others in the world?

B. **Holiness 102: Read Acts 2:1-13**
What does the fire of the Spirit empower the disciples to do? What impact does that have on the world?

C. **Victorious Living 201: Read 1 Corinthians 10:6-13**
How does God give you a "way out" when you are tempted to give up or sin? If you experienced victory every day in the Spirit, what impact would that have in your life?

D. **Victorious Living 202: Read Galatians 5:16-26**
If you were to "live by the Spirit," what fruit would be different in your life? How would that affect those who are close to you?

E. **The Future Revealed 101: Read Acts 16:6-10**
How did God reveal the future to Paul? What was God's purpose in giving Paul this vision?

You have a lifetime to experience the power and presence of the Holy Spirit as you study God's Word and get to know Him personally. He has many gifts waiting for you to open as you say, "Yes, I'll take that course!"

IV. THE SCHOOL OF THE FUTURE

A. **Another Amazing Class in the School of the Spirit**
There is another branch of God's School of the Spirit that I refer to as God's School of the Future. Can you imagine a class in which the teacher actually knows the future–an instructor who can teach history before it happens? The Holy Spirit knows it all! He intimately knows you! He is omniscient. Sometimes He wants to release preview clips of things to come for your personal life. He can do that! Yes, He can and does!

B. **A Surprising Page from My Life**
I distinctly remember one Sunday morning in May 1975, when I was 22 years old. I was taking one of my regular prayer walks with God, strolling through a park in Warrensburg, Missouri. Actually voicing the question aloud, as though I was talking with a friend walking beside me, I asked, "Who's for me?" What followed turned out to be a modern-day story just like those from the Bible. He answered and said, "Ann Willard." Skipping forward to the fulfillment of this word, I had the joy of being married to the wife of my youth for 32 years until her graduation to heaven in September 2008. God indeed knows the future of our personal lives.

C. The Spirit of Truth
He always points us in the right direction–toward truth. The Holy Spirit not only gives us a revelation of truth, but He also builds truthfulness into the depths of our personality.

V. THE ADVANTAGE IS GIVEN TO US

A. Jesus Is Always Right!
Jesus, the Son of God, who cannot lie, told His disciples that it was better for the Holy Spirit to come and be with them than for Him to remain. Jesus had more things to say to His disciples, but they could not take in any more right then. Jesus is always right.

B. Jesus Always Has a Way!
Jesus knew ahead of time that the disciples were going to need some ongoing coaching. He also knew He would have a lot more disciples to tutor in the centuries to come and that He could not carry on the job all by Himself. So the Master enacted a grand plan: He would go back to His Father, and they would send the Holy Spirit to the twelve disciples, to the other believers who were with them and to all subsequent disciples.

C. Isaiah 30:21
"Your ears will hear a word behind you, 'This is the way, walk in it,' whenever you turn to the right or to the left."

VI. HEAR HIS VOICE TODAY! CLOSING INVITATIONAL PRAYER
Father, I present myself to You in Jesus Christ's name. I declare that the Holy Spirit is alive and active in my life today. Draw me closer to Your heart so I can hear what the Spirit is saying. I ask that the Holy Spirit be my personal tutor, guide and teacher. I want to take more classes in Your School of the Spirit. Lead me. Guide me. Teach me how to listen more effectively, in Jesus Christ's name. Amen and Amen!

Reflection Questions
Lesson Two: The Holy Spirit at Work Today

Answers to these questions can be found in the back of the study guide.

Fill in the Blank

1. According to John 16:13, Jesus said when the Spirit has come, He will:
   a. _____
   b. _____
   c. _____
   d. _____

2. When our heavenly Father gave us the gift of Jesus, He gave us His very _____ in that one gift.

3. Another word for the Holy Spirit is the Holy _____.

Multiple Choice — Choose the best answer from the list below:

    A. Truth   C. Teacher
    B. Peace   D. Friend

4. Another definition for the word 'tutor' is _____.

5. The Holy Spirit is personal and always full of grace and _____

Continued on the next page.

True or False

6. The Holy Spirit always points us toward facts. _____

7. Jesus said it was better for Him to stay and remain with the disciples than for the Holy Spirit to come. _____

8. Isaiah 30:21 indicates you can hear a direction from God. _____

Scripture Memorization

9. Write out Isaiah 30:21 and memorize it.

Lesson Three:
The Sound of Many Rushing Waters

"Then I turned to see the voice that was speaking with me. And having turned I saw seven golden lampstands; and in the middle of the lampstands I saw one like a son of man, clothed in a robe reaching to the feet, and girded across His chest with a golden sash. His head and His hair were white like white wool, like snow; and His eyes were like a flame of fire. His feet were like burnished bronze, when it has been made to glow in a furnace,
and His voice was like the sound of many waters."
Revelation 1:12-15

"Behold, an angel of the Lord appeared to Joseph in a dream, and said, 'Get up! Take the Child and His mother and flee to Egypt, and remain there until I tell you; for Herod is going to search for the Child to destroy Him.'"
Matthew 2:13

"And the LORD opened the mouth of the donkey, and she said to Balaam, 'What have I done to you, that you have struck me these three times?' ...Then the LORD opened the eyes of Balaam, and he saw the angel of the LORD standing in the way with his drawn sword in his hand;
and he bowed all the way to the ground."
Numbers 22:28, 31

"But He answered and said, 'It is written, "Man shall not live on bread alone, but on every word that proceeds out of the mouth of God."'"
Matthew 4:4

Anne Morrow Lindbergh, a noted writer and aviation pioneer and the widow of aviator and conservationist Charles A. Lindbergh, Jr., once remarked, "Good communication is as stimulating as black coffee, and just as hard to sleep after."[8] How true that is! Have you ever come home from a date or a Bible study in which you've had an intense conversation and then tried to fall asleep? It's practically impossible.

I have stated it this way, "When God wants to speak, it's like trying to fall asleep after a triple espresso!"[9] Remember, God's life-giving Word proceeds and will continue to proceed. It is His ever-proceeding Word that gives us life! God has spoken; God is speaking; God will continue to speak and guide His children through the sound of many rushing waters.

Hearing and Obeying God's Voice
Lesson Three: The Sound of Many Rushing Waters

I. GOD STILL SPEAKS TODAY

A. The Proceeding Word
Deuteronomy 8:3 states, *"...man does not live by bread alone, but man lives by every word that proceeds out of the mouth of the Lord."* (AMP). This is quoted by Jesus in the Sermon on the Mount as recorded in Matthew 4:4.

The word *proceeds*, also found in Matthew 4:4, is a continuous-action verb. God's life-giving Word proceeds and continues to proceed.

B. The Confirming Words of Jesus
God confirms His Word by the testimony of two and three witnesses. It is His pattern in the Word of God and His pattern for each of our lives.

1. Deuteronomy 19:15
2. Matthew 18:6
3. 2 Corinthians 13:1

C. The Historical and Present-Tense, Living Jesus
It is wonderful to know the historical Jesus, who came in human form and walked among men. But God Himself yearns for us also to know the living, resurrected Christ through the present day power of the Holy Spirit. We have Good News! The Father wants to enable us to hear, know and obey the risen Lord.

II. A CHALLENGE THAT SHOOK ME!

A. An Early Lesson in My Journey
An early lesson that imprinted my spiritual life during the years of the Jesus Movement was that sometimes God speaks to us in different ways than we may be used to hearing him.

B. God's Voice Is Like a Radio
God has not quit speaking. He just switches channels on His dial. It's like God uses a radio when He speaks to us. He has just turned the knob over to a different channel or station on which you are not used to hearing Him. So we must be flexible to learn to hear Him in differing ways.

III. A TOOLBOX FULL OF TOOLS

A. An Assortment of Available Tools
1. A dream or vision (see Job 33:14-18)
2. A voice in a trance (see Acts 10:9-16)
3. The voice of many angels (see Revelation 5:11)
4. The voice of the archangel (see 1 Thessalonians 4:16)
5. The "sound of many waters" (see Revelation 1:15)
6. The sound of the Lord walking in the Garden (see Genesis 3:8)
7. The sound of the army of God marching in the tops of the trees (see 2 Samuel 5:23-25)
8. The audible voice of God (see Exodus 3:4)
9. God speaking peace to His people (see Psalm 85:8)
10. God's written Word, our primary source of His voice and our chief reference point (see Psalm 119:105)
11. Wonders in the sky and on earth (see Joel 2:30-31)
12. Visions and parables given to prophets (see Hosea 12:10)
13. Words and metaphors given to prophets (see Jeremiah 18:1-6)
14. The Holy Spirit speaking to a group (see Acts 13:2)
15. Men, moved by the Holy Spirit, declaring God's voice (see 2 Peter 1:21)
16. Heavenly experiences, in which one is brought up before the Lord (see 2 Corinthians 12:1-4)
17. The Holy Spirit bearing witness to our spirit (see Romans 8:16)
18. A dumb donkey speaking with the voice of a man (see 2 Peter 2:16)
19. One person speaking the revelatory counsel of the Lord to another (see James 5:19-20)
20. God's own Son (see Hebrews 1:2)[10]

IV. A PHONE CALL IN THE MIDDLE OF THE NIGHT

A. Another Personal Lesson in my Classes with the Holy Spirit
I received phone calls in the middle of the night in which no one answered on the other end. The Holy Spirit reminded me of Jeremiah 33:3, which says, *"Call to Me and I will answer you, and I will tell you great and mighty things, which you do not know."*

B. Quote from Author Quin Sherrer

"God speaks to us in many other ways. If we are open to hearing His voice at every turn, we will begin to recognize it with much greater frequency. Less dramatically, God can speak to us through an 'internal witness' or a 'knowing' in our innermost being, a settling peace, a conviction that the decision we might normally fret over is the right one. He can also speak through circumstances ('closed and open doors') or a seemingly serendipitous meeting that brings us an opportunity."[11]

V. GOD'S MULTIFACETED VOICE

A. Extraordinary Lessons from Psalm 29:3-9

1. *"The voice of the LORD is over the waters, the God of glory thunders"* (v. 3). Has God ever grabbed your attention in a dramatic way? How?

2. *"The voice of the LORD breaks the cedars; the LORD breaks in pieces the cedars of Lebanon"* (v. 5). Have you ever felt like you were "too dense" for the Lord to reach? Did God break through? How?

3. *"He makes Lebanon skip like a calf, Sirion like a young wild ox"* (v. 6). Have you ever needed to be refreshed by the Lord? Have you lost some of your zeal along the way? The intimacy of hearing His voice will make you skip once again.

4. *"The voice of the LORD hews out flames of fire"* (v. 7). Has God ever purified you with His Word? Why do you think God did that?

5. *"The voice of the LORD shakes the wilderness"* (v. 8). God will often shake our foundations to be sure that we have built our lives on a solid foundation. How has that happened to you?

B. Follow Through!

If you have heard His voice, now pause and take some time to thank the Lord and worship Him for the amazing invitation into the process of Hearing and Obeying His Voice Today!

VI. THE FINAL GOAL OF OUR LIVES

A. In Our Process of Becoming
In our process of becoming, we must not forget this is not just about us. It is about being transformed into the beautiful image of the glorious Lord Jesus Christ. By the power of the sound of many waters, which is our personal guide and tutor, the Holy Spirit, you and I will be changed into the image of God's Son.

B. Let the Voice of God Thunder!
Let the fire fall! Yes, everything in His temple shouts "Glory!" Come on, now. Do it with me. Give Him some praise, and watch what the Lord will do!

VII. WITH SHOUTS OF GLORY! CLOSING DECLARATIVE PRAYER

Lord, let Your voice be like the sound of many rushing waters in my life. Impart dreams and visions and an increase of the spirit of wisdom and revelation to me. Release Your angelic hosts to minister to me and my family. Open up Your written Word by that same spirit of wisdom and revelation. Turn the logos–the written Word–into a revelatory spoken word in my life. Open up new expressions of Your voice to me today. Amen and amen!

Reflection Questions
Lesson Three: The Sound of Many Rushing Waters

Answers to these questions can be found in the back of the study guide.

Fill in the Blank

1. List three of the twenty "tools' listed that God uses to speak to us:

    a. _____

    b. _____

    c. _____

2. "The Father wants to enable us to _____, _____, and _____ the risen Lord."

3. In Matthew 4:4, the word *proceeds* is a continuous action _____ and illustrates how God's live-giving Word proceeds and continues to _____.

Multiple Choice — Choose the best answer from the list below:

      A. Fire   C. Wilderness

      B. Cedars   D. Waters

4. According to Psalm 29:3, *"The voice of the Lord is over the _____."*

5. According to Psalm 29:8, *"The voice of the Lord shakes the _____."*

Continued on the next page.

True or False

6. In our process of becoming, it is about being conformed into the image of our Lord Jesus Christ. _____

7. The Holy Spirit is likened to the power of the sound of many waters. _____

8. Our personal guide and tutor in the process of being changed into the image of God's Son is the Holy Spirit. _____

Scripture Memorization

9. Write out Psalm 29:3 and memorize it.

Lesson Four:
Walking in Our Kingdom Birthright

"But you are a chosen race, a royal priesthood, a holy nation, a people for God's own possession, so that you may proclaim the excellences of Him who has called you out of darkness into His marvelous light."
1 Peter 2:9

"And He has made us to be a kingdom, priests to His God and Father–to Him be the glory and the dominion forever and ever. Amen."
Revelation 1:6

"For all who are being led by the Spirit of God, these are sons of God."
Romans 8:14

"If we live by the Spirit, let us also walk by the Spirit."
Galatians 5:25

As we have learned over the past few lessons, we not only have the right to speak to God, but also God desires to speak to us. As special objects of His divine nature, God will give direction, guidance, correction and love. But even when we understand that God wants to speak, we sometimes hesitate to listen. Why? What are the hindrances in the way?

Remember, hearing God's voice today is our birthright as a citizen of His Kingdom but is also a "long-term learning process." As you develop your ability to hear God's voice, don't be surprised if you find that God requires you to discover new ways to listen. It is always, "Listen and Obey!" This is true in my life and it will be in yours as well!

I. A PRIEST AND A PROPHET

A. Full Citizenship in a New Kingdom
Just as we have rights, privileges and responsibilities that come with our natural citizenship, we have the same in the spiritual realm. As citizens of the Kingdom of God, we have rights, privileges and responsibilities concerning the King of kings and Lord of lords. You and I are God's own possession, members of a chosen race!

B. Be A Priest First, then Turn Around and Be a Prophet!
1. A Priest represents the interests of the people before God.
2. A Prophet then represents the interests of God before the people. Just as we have the right as Kingdom citizens to make our appeals before the King, the King has the right to issue commands, decrees, desires and orders to His people.

C. Jack Deere — *Surprised by the Voice of God*
Scholar and theologian, Jack Deere, revealed in his classic book that the most difficult transition from his old kind of Christianity to a new and improved one was NOT learning to accept that God heals and does miracles today. Instead, the thing that took the most convincing, that he resisted the most and was most afraid of, was accepting the reality that God still *speaks* today.[12]

II. TAKING BABY STEPS AND FALLING DOWN!

A. An Embarrassing Moment!
In an early Jesus People Movement meeting I blurted, "Out of your innermost being shall come forth *livers* of living water!" The place erupted into laughter. I wanted to find an escape hatch in the floor somewhere so that I could quickly slip out of view. I corrected myself–"I mean *rivers*!"–but it was too late.

B. Shall I Go Hide and Quit?
I found this in Proverbs 24:16: *"For a righteous man falls seven times, and rises again."* I decided, God's people are not quitters, so neither was I going to be!

C. By the Grace of God!
I started learning it was more about a relationship with God than it was my success before man. I also learned it was all by the grace of God. So I continued to "Listen and Obey," to use His gift and respond to His call in spite of a few more bleeps, blunders and escapades. Through many trials and errors I learned there is no perfect start in hearing God's voice today, and I stepped back to the plate to eventually release His heart and His Word more accurately and effectively.

III. A FEW MORE STEPS ALONG THE WAY

A. Parallel Lessons from How Children Grow
When we are young in the Lord, our Papa God is there to speak to us in ways we can easily understand. Like young children, in the beginning stages, we need the directions spelled out really clearly for us. To hear those directions, each of us has a sweet spot in our heart to help us process. The Holy Spirit knows exactly where that sweet spot is and how to touch it, and He speaks right to it.

B. Growing Pains–Fewer Pat Answers!
Then, before we know it, we reduce what God has said into pat equations. But to keep us in a fresh love relationship with God, the Holy Spirit seems to change the rules without telling us.

Papa God speaks to us at our present level while at the same time always prodding us to move on, to grow up and mature. Our Father wants us to reach higher levels. To do so, we can't just keep communicating at our familiar level. We might go through some growing pains in the process. Remember, He can't forever be talking baby talk.

IV. SPEAK LESS, LISTEN MORE
Learning to hear God's voice today takes time–we can't leapfrog down the road the fast way. It takes many classes with many lessons. It takes patience, too!

A. Awakened in the Night Season
During the quiet hours of the night, night after night, I would be awakened by the Holy Spirit at 2:00 a.m. and would think, "Huh? I want to sleep! What are You doing?"

B. Responding to the Invitation
I learned to turn the ear of my spirit in His direction. I would get up out of bed and "sit with Him for a while." I did this for twenty years of my life, learning to simply be with Him without any agenda.

C. No Questions–Just Listening
One of the most common ways I hear from the Lord is simply by hearing the quiet inner voice of the Holy Spirit. God can and does speak to me in many ways, but He comes to me most often through His peaceful inner voice, which communes with my heart. This is when I just listen to Him, I let Him take the lead and share whatever is on His heart.

Hearing and Obeying God's Voice
Lesson Four: Walking in Our Kingdom Birthright

V. ARE YOU READY FOR A REVOLUTION?

A. The Revolution of the 1960's
About forty plus years ago, a new sound broke forth from England, and it quickly swept the world. A singing group called the Beatles took the nations by storm. Their simple, catchy lyrics captured hearts and promoted changes. One of their top songs was "Revolution." It helped throw an impressionable generation into a wild frenzy of drugs, free love and rebellion against authority.

B. It's Time for Change Once Again!
Now, over forty years later, another new sound can be heard. Another generation of people is discontented with the status quo. A radical yet intimate sound of prayer and worship is invading the Church and beginning to make a worldwide impact. I believe we are on the verge of a societal Holy Spirit revolution–a dramatic shift. Watch out, world; watch out, slumbering Church!

C. Dr. Michael Brown — Fire School
In his radical book *Revolution! The Call to Holy War*, Michael Brown declares, "Why is this dedication to a cause–this passionate, often selfless, sometimes murderous, always fanatical dedication–characteristic of revolutionary movements? It is because the revolutionary has an unshakable conviction that something is terribly wrong with society, that something very important is missing, that something major needs to change, indeed, that it must change now."[13]

VI. A BELIEVING BELIEVER — A PRAYER OF DESIRE
Dear Lord, I want to hear Your voice and learn Your ways. Be my teacher and guide. Enroll me in the School of the Spirit, and teach me to hear Your voice. Write down my name! I want to know You, to be a disciple of Christ Jesus, and to have sweet communion with You. I want to hear You, have more faith, and obey what You tell me. Help, Lord, for Your servant wants to listen. Amen and Amen!

Reflection Questions
Lesson Four: Walking in Our Kingdom Birthright

Answers to these questions can be found in the back of the study guide.

Fill in the Blank

1. As citizens in the Kingdom of God, you and I are the _____ of God, and members of a _____ race.

2. A _____ represents the interests of the people before God, and a _____ represents the interests of God before the people.

3. The King has the right to issue these four things to His people:
   a. _____
   b. _____
   c. _____
   d. _____

Multiple Choice — Choose the best answer from the list below:

    A. Restores   C. Blesses
    B. Heals   D. Speaks

4. One of the difficult transitions Jack Deere experienced as he left his old kind of Christianity was to believe that God still _____ and does miracles today.

5. The most radical change for Jack Deere, and the one he resisted the most was to believe the reality that God still _____ today.

Continued on the next page.

True or False

6. According to Proverbs 24:16, if a righteous man falls seven times he can finally stay down because it is wisdom at that point to give up. _____

7. Papa God speaks to us at our present level while at the same time always prodding us to grow up. _____

8. When it comes to interacting with God it is better to speak less and listen more. _____

Scripture Memorization

9. Write out 1 Peter 2:9 and memorize it.

Lesson Five:
Built Upon the Rock

"Thy Word is a lamp to my feet, and a light unto my path."
Psalm 119:105 KJV

"Everyone who comes to Me and hears My words and acts on them, I will show you whom he is like: he is like a man building a house, who dug deep and laid a foundation on the rock; and when a flood occurred, the torrent burst against that house and could not shake it, because it had been well built. But the one who has heard and has not acted accordingly, is like a man who built a house on the ground without any foundation; and the torrent burst against it and immediately it collapsed, and the ruin of that house was great."
Luke 6:47-49

"Be diligent to present yourself approved to God as a workman who does not need to be ashamed, accurately handling the word of truth."
2 Timothy 2:15

"Let the word of Christ dwell in you richly."
Colossians 3:16 NKJV

Have you ever experienced knowing you had to be at a certain place at a certain time, yet you only had a vague idea of how to get there; and instead of asking for directions, you just jumped into your car hoping everything would work out? What happened?

If you're experience has been like mine, sometimes this works out and sometimes it doesn't. You drive around frantically, saying to yourself, I know it's around here somewhere! I wish I had written down the directions before I left. Or when the wind and the waves hit your life you are left asking, Now, how I am going to make it through this? What will help me endure this storm?

Nobody likes the feeling of being lost or out of control. For many, the idea of listening to God's voice and understanding His will is a lot like trying to get somewhere without a blueprint or a map. We only have a vague idea of how to get the job done. But God has given us His directions on how to proceed in hearing His voice! His Will, His Word and His Ways are ever so solid and quite dependable, not only to get us to our next destination, but also as a foundation upon which to successfully build our lives.

I. KNOW YOUR COMPANION AND FRIEND

A. Guidance in the Word of God
The Bible is our roadmap, showing us which way to go. Without it, we could take a wrong turn on the road and double the length of time it takes to get to our destination. We need to get smarter! We need to take out the map and study it so we get to know the territory we are entering. We need to review the roadmap many times in order to end up at the right place, without running out of gas or even running off the road.

B. I Lost My Friend!
One time I misplaced my well-used Bible and could not find it. When I finally discovered it, I exclaimed, "I found my friend! I found my friend!"

C. Do You Have a Close Friend?
We each need a few close friends. But we also each need a special friend that speaks to us in a very personal manner. Do you have a special relationship with the Word of God in which you allow it to speak to you?

II. STORE UP THE WORD OF GOD

A. Hide God's Word in Your Heart!
We are admonished to hide God's Word in our hearts (see Psalm 119:11). As we do this consistently, we establish safety, security and protection for our lives. We then have a basis from which to judge the multitude of voices that come our way. We have a vast well of His words to draw from in times of need.

B. The Logos and the Rhema
The term *logos* (written word) is used 331 times in the Greek New Testament. The word *rhema* (spoken word) is used more than seventy times in the New Testament. In other words, *Logos* is used well over four times as often as is *rhema*, which helps us to see the relative importance of the logos, the sure foundation of the written Word of God.

C. The Relationship Between the Written and the Spoken Word
1. Planning (written) and execution (spoken)
2. Message (written) and vehicle (spoken)
3. Whole (written) and part (spoken)

III. HEAR THE WORD TO RELEASE FAITH

A. Faith Comes from Hearing
Romans 10:17 tells us, *"Faith comes from hearing [acoa in Greek], and hearing by the word [rhema] of Christ."* Acoa means "to have audience with, to come with ears."

B. The Importance of the Inner Attitude
How do we develop these important inner attitudes and expectancies that will determine how we hear and thus what we receive? Glancing again at Romans 10:17 – *"Faith comes from hearing"* – we see that our faith comes and continues to come by having an ongoing audience with God's words through the fellowship of the Holy Spirit.

C. Do You Want to Receive and Exercise Faith?
I want to receive and exercise faith. I know that faith pleases God. It enables me to live in new life. So, if I want to hear God's voice, I must come to God with my ears on. Will you do the same?

IV. MEDITATE ON THE WORD OF LIFE
We can read the Word. We can pray based on the words we read. But the approach to the Scriptures that will best help us to turn the logos into rhema is the spiritual discipline of meditating on the Word of Life.

A. The Lost Art of Practicing His Presence
In my book *The Lost Art of Practicing His Presence*, I attempt to dust off the art of Christian meditation and give some clarity to it. I wrote that the word *meditate* means "to think deeply or to reflect on something." To *reflect* on something means "to contemplate or ponder it." *Contemplate* means "to gaze at or think about intensely." [14]

B. From the Writings of Richard Foster — Meditative Prayer
"In Meditative Prayer the Bible ceases to be a quotation dictionary and becomes instead 'wonderful words of life' that lead us to the Word of Life. It differs even from the study of Scripture. Whereas the study of Scripture centers on exegesis, the meditation upon Scripture centers on internalizing and personalizing the passage. The written Word becomes a living word addressed to us."[15]

V. GOD'S GIVES DAILY MANNA TO HIS CHILDREN

A. Gathering Manna

1. Lessons from Exodus 16:4-5, 13-15
   "Then the LORD said to Moses, 'Behold, I will rain bread from heaven for you; and the people shall go out and gather a day's portion every day, that I may test them, whether or not they will walk in My instruction. On the sixth day, when they prepare what they bring in, it will be twice as much as they gather daily.'...

   "In the morning there was a layer of dew around the camp. When the layer of dew evaporated, behold, on the surface of the wilderness there was a fine flake-like thing, fine as the frost on the ground. When the sons of Israel saw it, they said to one another, 'What is it?' For they did not know what it was. And Moses said to them, 'It is the bread which the LORD has given you to eat.'"

2. Lessons from Exodus 16:16-19
   "This is what the LORD has commanded, 'Gather of it every man as much as he should eat; you shall take an omer apiece according to the number of persons each of you has in his tent.' The sons of Israel did so, and some gathered much and some little... He who had gathered much had no excess, and he who had gathered little had no lack; every man gathered as much as he should eat. Moses said to them, 'Let no man leave any of it until morning.'"

B. Applying Manna to Real Life

We must gather the Word as manna every day. Our portion today is only good for today. We cannot live off yesterday's manna. If we do not eat today's portion, we will have lack and need. But if we abide in His Word daily, we will have life within. That's the basic message here. We cannot live life today on yesterday's Word. By the same token, we cannot expect to hear God's *rhema* today when we haven't gathered in His *logos* yesterday or last week or last month, chewing it and digesting it. We can't get God's voice activated in our life today without first putting it into our hearts and minds.

VI. A LIFE BUILT UPON THE WORD — PRAYING THE WORD OF GOD

Father God, by the grace You supply, my life shall be built upon the rock of Your Word. I love the Word of God. The Bible is full of words of life for me. Teach me how to meditate upon and digest more of the amazing Word of God. I declare that I am growing in faith as I store up Your Word in my heart. I will hear what the Spirit is saying to me through the written Word. For Jesus Christ's sake, Amen.

Reflection Questions
Lesson Five: Built Upon the Rock

Answers to these questions can be found in the back of the study guide.

Fill in the Blank

1. According to Psalm 119:11, we are admonished to hide God's Word in our _____.

2. In Greek, the written word is known as _____ and the spoken word is known as _____.

3. What are the three phrases that illustrate the relationship between the Written and Spoken Word:
   a. _____ and _____
   b. _____ and _____
   c. _____ and _____

Multiple Choice — Choose the best answer from the list below:

    A. Feel   C. Speak
    B. Exercise   D. Hear

4. Faith comes when we _____ the Word (Rhema) of God.

5. It is very important to both receive and _____ faith.

Continued on the next page.

True or False

6. Meditating on God's Word is the spiritual discipline that will best help us to turn the rhema into logos. _____

7. In Exodus 16, The LORD caused bread to fall from heaven daily. _____

8. We must gather the Word of God once a week for our spiritual nourishment as the children of Israel did with the manna. _____

Scripture Memorization

9. Write out Colossians 3:16 and memorize it.

Lesson Six:
Ten Practical, Personal Tools

"Therefore everyone who hears these words of Mine and acts on them, may be compared to a wise man who built his house on the rock. And the rain fell, and the floods came, and the winds blew and slammed against that house; and yet it did not fall, for it had been founded on the rock."
Matthew 7:24-25

"Trust in the Lord with all your heart and lean do not lean on your own understanding. In all your ways acknowledge Him, and He will make your paths straight."
Proverbs 3:5-6

As we studied in the last lesson, knowing the Word of God and then speaking it into action generates faith for the Word to come to pass. As you spent time in God's written Word, did you experience a word of revelation from God?

This lesson presents ten practical and yet personal tools that will assist you in the art of hearing and the voice of God. As you apply these tools to your walk with God and put them into practice, they will make you a more effective follower in hearing and obeying God's voice.

I. THE HOLY SPIRIT IS THE FINGER OF GOD

A. Jesus Refers to the Holy Spirit as the Finger of God
"But if I cast out demons by the finger of God, then the kingdom of God has come upon you." Luke 11:20

B. The Personal Touch Only He Can Do
The Holy Spirit is called the finger of God. The finger points the way. The finger helps to personally identify who we are and Who God is. The finger releases a touch of tenderness. At the tip of a finger, there is a distinct design called the fingerprint. To effectively hear the voice of God today, we need the practical and personal work of the Holy Spirit expressed in His character and ways.

II. TEN PRACTICAL STEPS TO TAKE

Thus far, we have been laying a firm foundation upon which our house of God can be built. It is time to now learn from Jesus, our Master Carpenter, how to use ten tools that can assist us in the art of hearing and following God's voice today. It is time for us to be practical and pragmatic[16]. I encourage you to actively apply these relatable guidelines to your life.

A. Don't Make It Complicated
1. Submit to His Lordship
2. Resist the Enemy
3. Ask a Question and Expect God's Answer

B. Allow God to Speak How He Chooses
We should not try to dictate to God the guidance methods we prefer; rather, we must listen with a yielded heart.

C. Confess Any Known Sins
A clean heart is a prerequisite to hearing God. We read in Psalm 66:18, *"If I regard wickedness in my heart, the Lord will not hear."*

D. Obey the Last Thing God Said
Why would God give us new orders if we haven't obeyed His last one? He may be waiting for us to do what He's already told us to do.

E. Tune in to God's Voice
We need to become secure in our own identity in Christ. We must realize that we are sons and daughters of the Creator of the universe and that He wants to relate to us as unique children.

F. Don't Talk About It Too Soon!
1. The Trap of Pride
2. The Trap of Presumption
3. The Trap of Missed Timing
4. The Trap of Confusion

G. Know that God Will Confirm It
If it is really God speaking, He will speak the same or a similar thing more than once. 2 Corinthians 13:1: *"Every fact is to be confirmed by the testimony of two or three witnesses."*

H. Beware of Counterfeits
Satan loves to counterfeit. He is not the Creator, so he has no originality; he's just a copycat! Think about what a counterfeit means. It implies that there's something authentic and real out there, something worth copying.

I. Practice Hearing God's Voice

Yes, practice hearing the voice of God, and it will become easier. It's like picking up the phone and recognizing the voice of a friend, whose voice you know because you've heard it so many times.

J. Cultivate an Intimate Relationship

True guidance involves getting closer to the Guide. From God's perspective, the most important reason for hearing the voice of God is not so that we will know the right things to do, but so that we will know Him, the source of the guidance.

III. THE VOICE OF GOD CREATES HUNGER

The voice of God creates a deeper hunger within us so that we might come into closer communion with Him. The primary reason we need to hear His voice is really simple: to cultivate the intimate relationship with our Abba Father that He desires with us.

IV. SUBMITTING EVERY AREA — A PERSONAL PRAYER

Heavenly Father, I want a vibrant relationship with You that is both personal and practical. I choose to submit every area of my life to You. Release the finger of God–the Holy Spirit–to point out any hindrances in my life. Holy Spirit, bring me into Your marvelous light and lead me out of any dimensions of darkness. Come, Holy Spirit, and magnify the voice of God in my life today. Amen, and amen!

Reflection Questions
Lesson Six: Ten Practical, Personal Tools

Answers to these questions can be found in the back of the study guide.

Fill in the Blank

1. In Luke 11:20, Jesus refers to the Holy Spirit as the _____ of God.

2. A _____ heart is a prerequisite to hearing God.

3. List four traps to avoid when it comes to hearing God:
   a. _____
   b. _____
   c. _____ _____
   d. _____

Multiple Choice — Choose the best answer from the list below:

    A. Command   C. Speak
    B. Counterfeit   D. Boast

4. God will _____ the same or a similar thing more than once.

5. Because he is not the Creator, Satan loves to _____.

Continued on the next page.

True or False

6. Practice hearing the voice of God, and it will become easier. _____

7. The voice of God creates a deep sense of guilt within us. _____

8. The primary reason we need to hear the voice of God is to cultivate an intimate relationship with Him. _____

Scripture Memorization

9. Write out Proverbs 3:5-6 and memorize it.

Lesson Seven: Walking in Community

"If the foot says, 'Because I am not a hand, I am not a part of the body,' it is not for this reason any the less a part of the body. And if the ear says, 'Because I am not an eye, I am not a part of the body,' it is not for this reason any the less a part of the body. If the whole body were an eye, where would the hearing be? If the whole were hearing, where would the sense of smell be? But now God has placed the members, each one of them, in the body, just as He desired."
1 Corinthians 12:15-18

"A new commandment I give to you, that you love one another, even as I have loved you, that you also love one another. By this all men will know that you are My disciples, if you have love for one another."
John 13:34-35

In God's infinite wisdom, His primary vehicle of communication is through people. In fact, He became a person for just that reason. God demonstrated His love in the person of Jesus of Nazareth. And how did Jesus reveal God's love and will? He revealed God's love through His actions and words. We are to do the same.

We are His children, and we are supposed to look, act and talk like Him as His representatives on earth. But is the world able to see the Father's love in us? Moreover, can we see and hear our Papa God in and through our brothers and sisters? God lives in community. Do you? Do you have those who speak into your life and in whom you recognize the voice of God? This is one of the primary ways of hearing God's voice today.

I. A DIVERSE BODY

A. One of the Most Common Ways God Speaks
One of the most common ways the Lord speaks is through the members of the Body of Christ–each and every one. I think God must have fun at times as He attempts to speak to us through our spouses, parents, children and neighbors–especially the ones through whom we believe He surely wouldn't speak.

B. God Loves Diversity

We often set our own strict little boundaries about how and through whom God can speak to us. We tend to make a select list. Then, wham! Somebody messes with our list. We don't know what hit us, so we rebuke the devil. Later on, after we've become humbler, we learn it was God speaking to us in ways we didn't expect.

C. We Are His Body!

The Body of Christ has a diversity of parts, each one important to the whole. Read 1 Corinthians 12:12-27.

II. AN UNEXPECTED INVASION

In 1992, the presence of the Lord invaded our house for nine straight months. His angels came along with His manifested presence. The ensuing weeks of unusual divine encounters rocked our world, and the reverberations are still being felt today.

A. Beginning on the Day of Atonement

At 11:59 p.m. on the Jewish Day of Atonement, October 6, 1992, a heavenly visitor came and stood in our bedroom and spoke to me, "I have come to speak with your wife." In retrospect, I suppose that period was like a compressed "pregnancy" in the spirit, measured in weeks instead of months.

B. My Biggest Lesson Learned

Undoubtedly, as crazy as it may sound too many of you today, the biggest lesson I learned during those days was very simple, but it radically changed my perspective on God, relationships, husbands and wives. You ask, "What lesson was that, James?" I learned that God can speak to and through whomever He wants, whenever He wants.

C. Do You Know What This Means?

Maybe you–yes, you–are the next candidate God wants to invade with the glories of His brilliant presence!

III. UNCONVENTIONAL VESSELS

Those who are versed in the history of the Church realize that God has often spoken through unusual vessels. As we look back on it, this seemed to be the norm in scripture. But if Jesus showed up in person today, what would He look like?

IV. AN UNCOMFORTABLE WORD

A. Lessons from the Life of Naaman
Naaman was the captain of the army, a valiant warrior who served under the leadership of the king of Syria. He had a great reputation, except for one major problem–he was a leper. When he went to Elisha for healing, he became offended at what he was requested to do.

B. God Often Offends the Heart to Reveal
God always has a purpose behind an activity. We must learn to ask the right questions to get the right answers.

V. A SLEW (OR SLOUGH) OF BARRIERS

A. Common Obstacles to Hearing God's Voice:

1. Lack of faith
2. Lack of a strong commitment to Jesus as Lord
3. The presence of sin
4. Ignorance of the Scriptures
5. Lack of quality teaching
6. Fear of man and rejection
7. Fear of being deceived
8. Guilty feelings
9. Hurts from the past[17]

VI. AN OUTPOURING OF LOVE

A. The Law of Love Reads
"You shall love the Lord your God with all your heart, and with all your soul, and with all your strength, and with all your mind; and your neighbor as yourself." (Luke 10:27). When Jesus came, He didn't change that. He said, *"Do this, and you will live."* (verse 28).

B. Love Others as the Father Loved Jesus
We are to love one another as the Father loved Jesus. The mutual love that exists in the Godhead is our example. Do you want the world to hear the voice of God? His voice is most fully audible when brothers and sisters in Christ love each other (see John 13:15).

VII. ESTEEMING THE BODY OF CHRIST — PRAYING FOR HEALTHY COMMUNITY

Lord, I thank You for the Body of Christ and all those in spiritual authority. I thank You for my family members. Where I have a wrong independent spirit that causes me to run away from people and from You, please point it out to me. This day, I choose to esteem the many different members of the Body of Christ. I ask you to give me a healthy community of believers with whom to walk and from whom to learn. In Jesus' name, Amen.

Reflection Questions
Lesson Seven: Walking in Community

Answers to these questions can be found in the back of the study guide.

Fill in the Blank

1. In God's infinite wisdom, His primary vehicle of communication is through _____.

2. Of all the many diverse parts of the Body of Christ, each one is important to the _____.

3. God often speaks through _____ vessels.

Multiple Choice — Choose the best answer from the list below:

    A. Counseling   C. Embarrassed
    B. Offended   D. Healing

4. Naaman was a leper in needed of _____.

5. Elisha instructed Naaman on what he needed to do to be healed and Naaman was _____.

Continued on the next page.

True or False

6. The presence of sin is one the common barriers to hearing God. _____

7. Lack of seminary training will hinder you from hearing God. _____

8. Hurts from the past can be a barrier between us and God. _____

Scripture Memorization

9. Write out Luke 10:27-28 and memorize it.

Lesson Eight:
Hearing with Discernment

"A stranger they simply will not follow, but will flee from him, because they do not know the voice of strangers."
John 10:5

"Do not quench the Spirit; do not despise prophetic utterances. But examine everything carefully; hold fast to that which is good; abstain from every form of evil."
1 Thessalonians 5:19-22

"But solid food is for the mature, who because of practice have their senses trained to discern good and evil."
Hebrews 5:14

By taking some lessons in discernment we can avoid many common pitfalls in hearing God! This is a lot like driving a car. Instead of making the time to take driver's training classes, some people quickly get into the fastest car they can find and go off to the races. Some end up in ditches or become casualties of driving without a license. Some create problems with their zealous driving patterns and bump other cars off the road.

Let's avoid the ditches. Let's get our permits first, being mentored by an experienced driver sitting next to us, and then graduate to driving alone. Then let's repeat these safety lessons and help others with the very lessons we ourselves have learned. Where hearing God voice is concerned, "driver's education" includes lessons in discernment.

I.   THE NEED FOR DISCERNMENT
The gift of discerning of spirits, which is listed in the New Testament as one of the gifts of the Spirit (see 1 Corinthians 12:10), is desperately needed in today's church culture.

   A.   A Clear Definition from C. Peter Wagner
   The gift of discerning of spirits is the special ability that God gives to certain members of the Body of Christ to know with assurance whether certain behavior purported to be God is in reality divine, human or satanic (see 1 Corinthians 12:10; Acts 5:1-11; 16:16-18; 1 John 4:1-6; Matt. 16:21-23).[18]

B. Insights and Examples from Dr. Sam Storms

1. Acts 16:16-18, where Paul discerned that the power of a certain slave girl was, in fact, a demonic spirit
2. Acts 13:8-11, where Paul discerned that Elymas the magician was demonically energized in his attempt to oppose the presentation of the Gospel
3. Acts 14:8-10, where again Paul discerned ("saw") that a man had faith to be healed
4. When a person is able to discern whether or not a problem in someone's life is demonic or merely the consequence of other emotional and psychological factors, or perhaps a complex combination of both
5. When people with this gift are often able to detect or discern the presence of demonic spirits in a room or some such location
6. Acts 8:20-24, where Peter was said to "see" (not physically, but through perceiving or sensing) that Simon Magus was filled with bitterness and iniquity
7. It would seem that Jesus exercised something along the lines of this gift when he looked at Nathanael and described him as a man *"in whom there is no deceit"* (John 1:47). In John 2:25, it is said that Jesus *"knew what was in man."*[19]

C. Insights from the Prophet Isaiah

Isaiah the prophet, foreseeing the ministry of Jesus as the Messiah, the anointed one, declared that *"the spirit of the LORD...shall make him of quick understanding [literally, quick of scent] in the fear of the LORD: and he shall not judge after the sight of his eyes, neither reprove after the hearing of his ears."* (Isaiah 11:2-3 KJV). Those to whom God commits the care of His sheep must likewise, through the Holy Spirit, be quick of scent.

II. THREE SOURCES OF REVELATION

The Scriptures teach us that spiritual revelation or communication comes from one of three sources: the Holy Spirit, the human soul or the realm of evil spirits.

A. The Holy Spirit Is the Only True Source

"No [true] prophecy was ever made by an act of human will, but men moved by the Holy Spirit spoke from God." (2 Peter 1:21). The Greek word for "moved", *phero*, means "to be borne along or even to be driven along as a wind."

B. Second Source–The Human Soul
Thoughts, ideas and inspirations that don't originate with the Holy Spirit can be voiced by the human soul–the second source. These come out of the unsanctified portion of our emotions (see Jeremiah 23:16 and Ezekiel 13:1-6).

C. Third Source–Demonic Evil Spirits
The third source of revelation, evil spirits, can appear to be angels of light (good voices), but they always speak lies because they serve the chief liar and father of lies, Satan. Consider the slave girl with a spirit of divination described in Acts 16. She spoke the truth about the disciples, but she got her information from a satanic source.

III. NINE TESTS OF REVELATION
Since the Bible is our absolute standard against which we must test spiritual experiences, let's look at nine scriptural tests. I adapted these solid guidelines years ago into my own style from the ministry of the great British Bible teacher Derek Prince.

A. Does the Revelation Edify, Exhort or Console?
The end purpose of all true revelation is to build up, admonish and encourage the people of God (see 1 Corinthians 14:3).

B. Is It in Agreement with God's Word?
"All Scripture is given by inspiration of God." (2 Timothy 3:16 NKJV). Where the Holy Spirit has said yes and amen in Scripture, He also says yes and amen in revelation. He never contradicts Himself.

C. Does It exalt Jesus Christ?
"He will glorify Me, for He will take of Mine and will disclose it to you." (John 16:14). All true revelation centers on the person of Jesus Christ and exalts Him (see Revelation 19:10).

D. Does It Have Good Fruit?
"Beware of the false prophets, who come to you in sheep's clothing, but inwardly are ravenous wolves. You will know them by their fruits." (Matthew 7:15-16). The true voice of God will produce fruit in character and conduct that agrees with the fruit of the Holy Spirit (see Galatians 5:22-23 and Ephesians 5:9).

E. If It Predicts a Future Event, Does It Come to Pass?
"When a prophet speaks in the name of the LORD, if the thing does not come about or come true, that is the thing which the LORD has not spoken. The prophet has spoken it presumptuously; you shall not be afraid of him." (Deuteronomy 18:22).

F. Does the Revelation Turn People Toward God or Away from Him?
If a person's words seem to be accurate but end up turning people away from following Jesus Christ as the Son of God, then it is a mistake to adhere to his or her ministry. (See Deuteronomy 13:1-5)

G. Does It Produce Liberty or Bondage?
True revelation given by the Holy Spirit produces liberty, not bondage (see 1 Corinthians 14:33 and 2 Timothy 1:7).

H. Does It Produce Life or Death?
"For the letter kills, but the Spirit gives life." (2 Corinthians 3:6). The authentic voice of God always produces growth and life-giving energy, not hopelessness, stagnation or defeat.

I. Does the Holy Spirit Bear Witness that It Is True?
The Holy Spirit is called "the Spirit of truth" (John 16:13). His indwelling presence in our hearts and minds provides us with a kind of supernatural common sense about the accuracy of words that seem to be from God. This ninth test is the most subjective and therefore should always be used in conjunction with the previous eight standards.

IV. THE NEED FOR SURRENDERED SENSES

A. Presenting Our Members to the Holy Spirit

1. Surrendering our Senses to the Holy Spirit
   This involves the very act of presenting the members of our physical body to God (see Romans 6:13, 19). To whomever we present our members, to them they become a slave. So, let's present our entire being unto God as an act of worship (see Romans 12:1-2).

2. This Act of Presentation Is So Very Vital
   It is a key to accurately moving in a higher realm of the anointing of the Holy Spirit. Surrendering and presenting our natural five senses to the Dove of God is a very specific and necessary part of the process.

B. Practice Training Sessions

1. The Model from Hebrews 5:14
   Hebrews 5:14 says, *"But solid food is for the mature, who because of practice have their senses trained to discern good and evil."* This is about the training of our senses, which help us discern. They are a key component of the process.

2. Practice Is a Normal Aspect of any Learning Process
   This is part of your maturation as a disciple of Jesus, which always stems from Bible study, experience and discipline. Don't forget–you can always ask God to give you more ability to discern spirits and to grow into greater maturity. He wants this for us more than we want it ourselves!

V. TEACH ME TO DISCERN — A PRAYER ASKING FOR WISDOM

Father God, Your Word tells me to not despise prophesying, to test all things and to hold fast to what is good. Teach me to discern Your voice. I lift up Your Word as my standard. Help me to be a wise steward of Your grace, dear Lord. Teach me to discern good from evil. Grant me an appropriate fear of You and the wisdom to judge revelation properly. In Jesus' mighty name, Amen.

Reflection Questions
Lesson Eight: Hearing with Discernment

Answers to these questions can be found in the back of the study guide.

Fill in the Blank

1. The gift of _____ ____ _____ is one of the gifts of the Spirit in 1 Corinthians 12:10 desperately needed today.

2. According to insights from Dr. Sam Storms, people with this gift are able to _____ or discern the presence of demonic spirits in a location.

3. The Scriptures teach us that spiritual revelation comes from one of these three sources:
   a. _____
   b. _____
   c. _____

Multiple Choice — Choose the best answer from the list below:

    A. Complements   C. Agrees
    B. Competes   D. Exalts

4. One of the tests of revelation is to see if it _____ with the Word of God.

5. Another test of revelation is it _____ the Lord Jesus Christ.

Continued on the next page.

True or False

6. Presenting our entire being to God is an act of worship. _____

7. The training of our physical bodies helps us in discernment. _____

8. Practice is a normal aspect of any learning process. _____

Scripture Memorization

9. Write out Hebrews 5:14 and memorize it.

Lesson Nine:
He Will Guide You!

"Although the Lord has given you the bread of privation and water of oppression, He, your Teacher will no longer hide Himself, but your eyes will behold your Teacher. Your ears will hear a word behind you, 'This is the way, walk in it,' whenever you turn to the right or to the left."
Isaiah 30:20-21

"Your word is a lamp to my feet and a light to my path."
Psalm 119:105

"But when He, the Spirit of truth, comes, He will guide you into all the truth; for He will not speak on His own initiative, but whatever He hears, He will speak; and He will disclose to you what is to come."
John 16:13

Do you remember playing the Hot or Cold game as a child? You would be blindfolded, and some object in the room would be selected by the others for you to try to find as you blindly groped around the room. Your playmates would shout, "You're getting warmer! No, you're cold. Warm...warmer...hot!" Of course, hot meant you were getting closer to the desired object, and cold meant you were going in the wrong direction.

Are you getting warmer–closer to what God wants to say? Or are you getting colder–further away from it? Do you pay attention to the signals? How well do you navigate the maze of voices vying for your attention? The following principles will guide you along your way.

I. THE GEIGER COUNTER OF GUIDANCE

A. The Geiger Counter Explained
The Geiger counter is an interesting instrument named for Hans Geiger, the German physicist who invented it in 1928. The Geiger counter can detect the presence and intensity of radiation (the spontaneous emission of energy from radioactive elements, most notably uranium) by using a gas-filled tube that briefly conducts electricity when radiation makes the gas conductive.

The Geiger counter amplifies this signal into a series of clicks. The closer it gets to the radioactive substance and the greater the intensity of the substance's radiation, the louder and faster the clicking noise becomes.

B. Our Approach to Hearing God's Voice

Our spirit is like the Geiger counter that tells us whether we are closer or further away. It helps us put all the pieces together. We learn to pay attention to an inner witness. We check in with the Holy Spirit, we listen to our "knower," and our spirit either bears witness or it doesn't.

When we are filled with the Holy Spirit, we have a divine guidance system that comes as part of the package, and we need that guidance system to get to the right result.

II. TEN PRINCIPLES OF DIVINE GUIDANCE

Some of the principles may be review for you, and some may be fresh and new. Let these ten principles of divine guidance help you hear God's voice today, determine His guidance and, most of all, grow closer to God Himself.

A. Principle 1: The Will of God Is Made Known in the Word of God

Some people start trying to listen to the subjective (listening for an inner voice) without first being grounded in the objective (the Word of God). They don't have a gauge to judge what they're sensing, hearing, feeling, thinking, or what I call knowing. In all guidance, God's Word is the final judge. Let God's Word have the final say.

B. Principle 2: The Will of God Is Confirmed through Circumstances

Circumstances alone don't constitute divine guidance, but they can often confirm God's will. Do not use this principle as your sole source of guidance, but know that it is one of the long term ways of the Holy Spirit to confirm His direction in our lives.

C. Principle 3: The Holy Spirit Speaks from Where He Dwells

Where does God dwell? Not only does He dwell in heaven, but He also dwells within us if we are children of God who have been filled with the Holy Spirit. According to 1 Corinthians 6:19, *"Your body is a temple of the Holy Spirit who is in you."* Colossians 1:27 confirms, *"Christ in you, the hope of glory."* He speaks to us from where He dwells, which is in us.

D. Principle 4: Divine Guidance Comes from Meeting God's Conditions

What are the divine conditions that must be met for guidance to be unlocked? Has He heard our cry? If we meet His conditions, He will surely guide us.

E. **Principle 5: The Peace of God Accompanies True Guidance**
According to Romans 14:17, *"The kingdom of God is not eating and drinking, but righteousness and peace and joy in the Holy Spirit."* If God's voice is an instrument of His Kingdom, then His voice speaks peace, not chaos.

F. **Principle 6: Much Guidance from God Comes Unnoticed**
When it comes to this realm of divine guidance, humility is another subtle key that unlocks God's provision: *"He leads the humble in justice, and He teaches the humble His way."* (Psalm 25:9)

G. **Principle 7: Divine Guidance Does Not Mean We Know All the Details**
Most of the time, we will see what is in front of us. That's just the way it is. It keeps us humble and reliant on God. Go with what the lamp of God's word is already revealing, and His light will give you more every step of the way.

H. **Principle 8: The Process of Guidance Is Not Always Pleasant**
Isaiah 55:8-9 tells us that God's thoughts are higher than ours. Sometimes the voice of the Lord and His guidance system is like that proverbial sand in the oyster. At the beginning it can seem like an irritant. But give it some time and room to do its work, and a pearl of great price will emerge. If we choose His way over our way, it might seem painful for the moment, but the end result will be good.

I. **Principle 9: Hearing God Speak Should Prompt Us to Action**
God's word is compelling. If we act on it, we'll hear more. In Daniel 11:32 we read, *"But the people who know their God will display strength and take action."*

J. **Principle 10: Guidance Is a Skill to Be Learned over a Lifetime**
If we have heard God speak once, we cannot assume we've learned how to hear Him once and for all. We are on a lifetime walk with Him. There are always more classes to take in the School of the Spirit that teach us to hear God's voice today.

III. LEANING UPON THE HEART OF GOD

To really grow in the very subjective art of hearing God for myself, I need to be like John the beloved and lean my head upon the chest of my Messiah and Master, listening for the very heartbeat of God. You and I need to cultivate a friendship with Jesus. Then we will be able to hear God in all His multifaceted modes of expression.

We will find that true guidance is not just a one-time thing. Hearing the voice of God depends on having a lifetime relationship, and that can never be taken away. It is walking with the Guide Himself.

IV. GUIDE ME INTO YOUR WILL — A PRAYER FOR DIVINE GUIDANCE

Lord, I want to be led by Your Spirit and hear Your voice speaking more clearly. Tune me to Your voice. Grant me the supernatural ability to discern Your voice from the voice of the stranger. Guide me. Be my navigation system to help me through the maze of life so that I get to where You want me to be and do what You want me to do. Lead me and guide me in Your will and Your ways. In Jesus' great name, Amen.

Reflection Questions
Lesson Nine: He Will Guide You!

Answers to these questions can be found in the back of the study guide.

Fill in the Blank

1. Our spirits are like the _____ _____ in that it tells us whether we are closer or further away in regard to hearing the voice of God.

2. List the first three (of the ten) principles of divine guidance:
   a. _____
   b. _____
   c. _____

3. Principles of divine guidance, number four states: "Divine guidance comes from meeting God's _____."

Multiple Choice – Choose the best answer from the list below:

   A. Justice   C. Grace
   B. Righteousness   D. Kindness

4. *"The kingdom of God is not eating and drinking, but _____, peace and joy in the Holy Ghost."* (Romans 14:17)

5. *"He leads the humble in _____, and He teaches the humble His way."* (Psalms 25:9)

Continued on the next page.

True or False

6. Divine guidance means we know all the details. _____

7. The process of (divine) guidance is first and foremost pleasant. _____

8. Divine guidance is a skill to be learned over a lifetime. _____

Scripture Memorization

9. Write out Isaiah 30:20-21 and memorize it.

Lesson Ten: Listening, Waiting and Watching

"The Lord God has given Me the tongue of disciples, that I may know how to sustain the weary one with a word. He awakens Me morning by morning; He awakens My ear to listen as a disciple. The Lord God has opened My ear; and I was not disobedient nor did I turn back."
Isaiah 50:4-5

*"Those who wait for the Lord will gain new strength; they will mount up with wings like eagles, they will run and not get tired,
they will walk and not become weary."*
Isaiah 40:31

"I will stand on my guard post and station myself on the rampart; and I will keep watch to see what He will speak to me, and how I may reply when I am reproved. Then the Lord answered me and said, "Record the vision and inscribe it on tablets that the one who reads it may run. For the vision is yet for the appointed time; it hastens toward the goal and it will not fail. Though it tarries, wait for it; for it will certainly come, it will not delay."
Habakkuk 2:1-3

Hearing God's voice today is a very natural act but requires the activity of a supernatural God. There is no automatic-pilot setting that guarantees that you will hear. One truth is that if you do nothing, you will receive nothing. But the seeming opposite is also true: When you least qualify and least expect it, God shows up! While I emphasize that all good things come by grace, I also teach that we must add works to our faith to be effective (see James 2:26). These are two sides of the same coin.

Yes, hearing God's voice today includes some basic dos and don'ts, but it is not about a list of deeds to be done out of religious obligation. Hearing God's life-changing voice is an amazing privilege based in a loving relationship with our heavenly Father. It is a delight and an honor, not a religious act built on some performance-based acceptance.

I. THREE KEY INVITATIONS

The following passage has guided my life with Papa God for many years and can provide you with further tools, as well, when it comes to this relational art form of communing with God and hearing His voice today:

"Now therefore, O sons, listen to me, for blessed are they who keep my ways. Heed instruction and be wise, and do not neglect it. Blessed is the man who listens to me, watching daily at my gates, waiting at my doorposts. For he who finds me finds life and obtains favor from the LORD." Proverbs 8:32-35, emphasis added

A. In the Life of Joshua

Moses chose young Joshua for a long apprenticeship, through which he became a steward of the promises given to one generation and fulfilled in the next generation.

According to Exodus 33:7-11, Joshua was schooled in art of waiting, listening, and watching daily at the gates. He observed firsthand the lessons related to hearing God's voice and encountering the fiery presence of God. This set Joshua aside from others and postured him to be an inheritor of the promises of the preceding generation.

B. In the Life of David

Few people could say they were a psalmist, a shepherd of the flocks, a warrior, a prophet and a king, but David could. I wonder if his harp-and-bowl ministry before the Lord is what caught the Father's eye. Could that be why the Scriptures say David had God's own heart (see Acts 13:22)?

C. In the Life of My Bride

One of my fondest memories of my time with Michal Ann happened in the last three months of her life on this side of heaven. I remember the early morning when, in her weakened state, we sat together in our rocking chairs on the front porch of our southern house, drinking organic green tea. We said nothing the entire time; we just listened. "Just listened?" To what?

Oh, to the sounds of silence. We listened to the morning dew glistening on the grass. We listened to the sun rising. We watched the rays of light melt away the fog on our pond at a distance down the hill. This was her way and this was her life. Listening, waiting and watching for the very movement of the dove of God.

II. KEEP ON LISTENING

So, yes, keep on listening. When you take time to shut the door and commune with God, you will hear wonderful words of life–wonderful words meant for you and you alone.

A. Key Scripture—Isaiah 50:4-5

"The Lord GOD has given me the tongue of a disciple, that I may know how to sustain the weary one with a word. He awakens Me morning by morning, He awakens my ear to listen as a disciple. The Lord GOD has opened My ear; and I was not disobedient, nor did I turn back."

Ask that you be given a listening ear. Declare that He has given you the tongue of a disciple as a result of having an awakened ear.

B. Key Scripture—Mark 9:1-8

"Then a cloud formed, overshadowing them, and a voice came out of the cloud, 'This is My beloved Son, listen to Him!'" (Mark 9:7-8)

In order to hear God, we must learn to deal with distraction. The key is to be so focused on Him that everything else fades into the background.

III. KEEP ON WATCHING

So, yes, keep on watching. Watching could be considered both a gift and an art that must be learned. The proper inner attitude is the key that unlocks our ability to hear and see in the Spirit.

A. Key Scripture—Habakkuk 2:1-3

"I will stand on my guard post and station myself on the rampart; and I will keep watch to see what He will speak to me, and how I may reply when I am reproved. Then the LORD answered me and said, 'Record the vision and inscribe it on tablets, that the one who reads it may run. For the vision is yet for the appointed time; it hastens toward the goal and it will not fail. Though it tarries, wait for it; for it will certainly come, it will not delay.'"

B. Key Scripture—Matthew 26:40

"Could you not watch with Me one hour?" NKJV

C. Key Scripture—Ezekiel 33:6

"But if the watchman sees the sword coming and does not blow the trumpet and the people are not warned, and a sword comes and takes a person from them, he is taken away in his iniquity; but his blood I will require from the watchman's hand."

IV. KEEP ON WAITING

So, yes, keep on waiting. He waits for us. He longs for us. He yearns to demonstrate His deep-seated compassion toward us. He comes running when He hears our voice!

A. Key Scripture—Isaiah 30:18-21

"Therefore the LORD longs to be gracious to you, and therefore He waits on high to have compassion on you. For the LORD is a God of justice; how blessed are all those who long for Him. O people in Zion, inhabitant in Jerusalem, you will weep no longer. He will surely be gracious to you at the sound of your cry; when He hears it, He will answer you. Although the Lord has given you bread of privation and water of oppression, He, your Teacher will no longer hide Himself, but your eyes will behold your Teacher. Your ears will hear a word behind you, 'This is the way, walk in it,' whenever you turn to the right or to the left."

B. Key Scripture—Mark 16:17-18

"These signs will accompany (follow) those who have believed: in My name they will cast out demons, they will speak with new tongues; they will pick up serpents, and if they drink any deadly poison, it will not hurt them; they will lay hands on the sick, and they will recover."

V. LESSONS FROM ANDREW MURRAY — WAITING ON GOD

"We must not only think of our waiting upon God, but also of what is more wonderful still, of God's waiting upon us. The vision of Him waiting on us will give new impulse and inspiration to our waiting upon Him. It will give us an unspeakable confidence that our waiting cannot be in vain. If He waits for us, then we may be sure that we are more than welcome–that He rejoices to find those He has been seeking for. Let us seek even now, at this moment, in the spirit of lowly waiting on God, to find out something of what it means. Therefore, will the Lord wait, that He may be gracious unto you. We will accept and echo back the message: Blessed are all they that wait for Him."

VI. SITTING AT YOUR FEET — A PRAYER TO BE A GOOD STEWARD

Father, in Jesus' great name, I thank You for graduate-level classes that are available for me in the School of the Spirit. Impart to me greater grace to enjoy these spiritual privileges. I count it an honor and blessing to be welcomed into Your presence; to sit at Your feet and listen to Your every word. Help me to be a good steward of these truths. Amen and amen!

Reflection Questions
Lesson Ten: Listening, Waiting and Watching

Answers to these questions can be found in the back of the study guide.

Fill in the Blank

1. According to Exodus 33:7-11, Joshua was schooled in the art of three things each day:
   a. _____
   b. _____
   c. _____

2. *"He (the Lord GOD) awakens me morning by morning; He awakens my ear to listen as a _____."* (Isaiah 50:4b)

3. In order to hear God, we must learn to deal with _____.

Multiple Choice – Choose the best answer from the list below:

A.	Watching	C.	Listening
B.	Wait	D.	Pray

4. _____ could be considered both a gift and an art that must be learned.

5. According to Habakkuk 2:3, we are to _____ for the vision that the LORD will give at the appointed time.

Continued on the next page.

True or False

6. In Ezekiel 33:6, the blood of the people that were not warned by the watchman will be required of him. _____

7. Isaiah 30:18 tells us that there are times that the LORD waits to be gracious to us. _____

8. Mark 16:17-18 describes signs that will follow all those that believe in His name. _____

Scripture Memorization

9. Write out Habakkuk 2:1-3 and memorize it.

Lesson Eleven:
Properly Responding to God's Voice

"For He is God, and we are the people of His pasture and the sheep of His hand. Today, if you would hear His voice, do not harden your hearts."
Psalm 95:7-8

"Today if you hear His voice, do not harden your hearts, as when they provoked Me."
Hebrews 3:15b

"This command I entrust to you, Timothy, my son, in accordance with the prophecies previously made concerning you, that by them you fight the good fight."
1 Timothy 1:18

There is hearing God's voice and there is responding to God's voice. These are two interdependent sides of the same truth. Passivity is not even close to being a proper response to God and His word. God is moved by faith and by people who take action (see Daniel 11:32). We must be actively engaged in seeking the Lord for the conditions–whether spoken or not yet revealed–that must be met in order to unlock the promises He has given.

On one hand we have the promise revealed, and on the other side of the coin we have the promise fulfilled. Another way of saying it is, we have the promise offered and then we need to see the promise manifested. The problem is that there is a gap between these polar opposite positions which I call the "until clause." So let's venture forth as I attempt to address what to do between the promise and its fulfillment in this lesson on Properly Responding to God's Voice.

I. LEARNING FROM BIBLICAL PRECEDENT

So how are we, as believers, supposed to respond in these transitional phases? We are not meant to stay in the valley, throw up our hands, resign, give up or just sit there. No! We must learn the ways of properly responding to the voice of God, thus contending for the promise in order to step into our Promised Land. Let's take a look at two Biblical examples.

A. Lessons from the Life of Jacob
Genesis 32:24-29 gives us the history lesson of Jacob wrestling with an angel all night long. He would not let the angel go "until he had received the blessing." What was Jacob doing wrestling with an angel anyway? Why and what for?

I am convinced that this story contains a dimension of contending for the promise that we need to emulate. Most of us could use more of Jacob's tenacious attitude and gutsy approach when it comes to seeing God's stated-promises fulfilled. It is my belief that our good, heavenly Father wants to bless us richly. He rewards diligence and faith and He invites us into the process of hearing and responding to His Voice.

B. Lessons from the Life of Daniel

Daniel meditated on the promises revealed to Jeremiah that the Israelites' captivity would come to an end after seventy years of exile (see Daniel 9:1-2). Daniel responded to this promise of the Lord by praying to see if there were any hindrances standing in the way of their fulfillment. Then in Daniel 10:12-14 we are given the following glimpse into activities behind the scenes.

"Then he said to me, 'Do not be afraid, Daniel, for from the first day that you set your heart on understanding this and on humbling yourself before your God, your words were heard, and I have come in response to your words. But the prince of the kingdom of Persia was withstanding me for twenty-one days; then behold, Michael, one of the chief princes, came to help me, for I had been left there with the kings of Persia. Now I have come to give you an understanding of what will happen to your people in the latter days, for the vision pertains to the days yet future.'"

C. Lessons from the Lives of Jacob and Daniel Brought Together

In these Biblical precedents from the lives of both Jacob and Daniel, we find two different but complimentary prerequisites. With Jacob we find tenacious contending. On the opposite side, from Daniel we find humble contrition and confessing generational sins. We need both postures brought together as tools of contending to bring forth God's promises.

II. WHY CONTENDING IS NECESSARY

The following principles are tools of understanding to keep you moving forward and avoiding ruts.

A. It's Not Just for You

Your personal victory builds a testimony, which in turn helps others receive strength and encouragement to persevere, too. You might also be contending for deliverance for your entire family, church culture, city and nation. Come on, now. You are contending for more than just yourself!

B. It Strengthens You in God
In the ways of God, contending spiritually is a lot like lifting weights—there is a resistance factor that eventually works in your favor. Your tenacious response causes you to grow up spiritually, tests your motivations and builds you up. Contending builds you up!

C. It Threatens the Enemy
Why is contending necessary? Because we have a real enemy, and your success is a threat to the kingdom of darkness. Your fulfilled dream is one of the enemy's worst nightmares!

D. It Takes a Team Working Together
Often, fulfilling the Lord's invitation does not just depend on us; it involves the will, attitude and fortitude of others also. Some people, churches, cities and nations give up too soon. When they are at the brink of crossing over from promises revealed to promises fulfilled, they quit. Not on my watch! Remember, together in Jesus, we make a great team!

III. HOW TO KEEP MOVING FORWARD
Contending for a promise long after it has been released involves perseverance. At times, it takes all of the strength we have to continue. But we must never, never quit! With this in mind, here are some ways I have found to keep going when the road grows long.

A. Walk in Faith
All progress in the Christian life is made through faith. We walk by faith and not by sight (see 2 Corinthians 5:7). Also, please note that God rewards those who diligently seek Him, and He rewards faith (see Hebrews 11:6).

B. Receive and Release
Do you want to move forward in your personal or corporate destiny in God? Then realize you are part of a relational community—or, at least, you should be. This means that you must learn to receive God's great love, grace and forgiveness and then turn around and demonstrate those same Kingdom principles to others.

C. Belong to Others
According to 1 John 5:4, *"For whatever is born of God overcomes the world; and this is the victory that has overcome the world—our faith."* Take note, this verse does not state *"my faith."* It implicitly states *"our faith."* We overcome the world by our faith.

D. Behold His Face
We are engaged in a love war. Look into God's face. Get yourself in front of Him. How do we keep moving forward? By engaging in the art of beholding. You become like what (or whom) you behold.

E. Sacrifice to Release Power
Today's sacrifice releases tomorrow's privilege and provision. Today's humility releases greater grace for your future (see James 4:6). What you do matters, and how you live determines your outcome. Little acts of sacrifice release heaven's response.

F. Pursue Fresh Vision
According to Proverbs 29:18, without a progressive vision, the people perish. Are you keeping God first? Are you seeking first His kingdom and His righteousness (see Matthew 6:33)? Are you keeping the authentic, confirmed, revealed promise in front of your eyes? You can do this through journaling, declaring the promise and many other ways.

G. Journal to Steward Revelation
Do you need assistance retaining what you have received? There is a simple solution for you–journaling! Yes, it is one of the spiritual privileges I referred to earlier. Journaling is a tried-and-tested spiritual tool for stewarding revelation that can aid you in discerning the voice of the Holy Spirit.

H. Lean into Perseverance
Persevere. It will pay off. The promise will come. You will move from promise revealed to promise fulfilled. Just don't quit. If I had one key in life, it would be called old-fashioned perseverance, and I want you to possess that same key, too.

IV. WHAT YOU CAN KNOW FOR SURE
In order to succeed in life and ministry, some basic, fundamental decisions must be applied every time–no matter what.

A. Say Yes to the Lord
1. Focus your faith on the Giver, not the gift (see Hebrews 11:6).
2. Hold on to the words God has given with "open expectancy."
3. Be thankful for what you've received. We are to not despise God's words (see 1 Thessalonians 5:20).
4. Follow Daniel's example and pray the promise into existence (see Jeremiah 29:10; Daniel 9).
5. Fight the good fight of faith–do spiritual battle according to the word from the Lord (see 1 Timothy 1:18).

B. Say No to Ourselves
1. Put down fantasy and unrestrained speculation, bringing every thought captive to Christ Jesus (see 2 Corinthians 10:5).
2. Embrace discipleship and the death-and-resurrection process (see John 12:24).
3. Exercise patience! There are no shortcuts with God.
4. Learn to give grace and mercy to others, as we are all still in training.

V. HOW TO RESPOND IN DRY SEASONS

If you find yourself in a dry place, consider some of the following proper responses:

A. Stick with What You Already Know
B. Consider That You Might Be in a Test–Will You Pass It?
C. Don't Doubt in Darkness What You Have Seen or Heard in Times of Light
D. Don't Compare Yourself to Others
E. Be Childlike–Don't Overly Complicate Things!

VI. LISTEN AND OBEY — A PRAYER FOR PROPER STEWARDSHIP

Father God, I am grateful for the progress we are making together. Thank You for enrolling me in these graduate-level classes on hearing and discerning Your voice. Help me to properly respond to Your whispers, dreams, visitations and various encounters. I want to listen and obey! Lead me by Your grace into greater applications of these spiritual privileges. In Jesus' great name, Amen.

Reflection Questions
Lesson Eleven: Properly Responding to God's Voice

Answers to these questions can be found in the back of the study guide.

Fill in the Blank

1. In order to step into our Promised Land, we must learn ways of properly _____ to the voice of God.

2. According to Genesis 32:24-29, Jacob would not let the angel when he was wrestling him "until he had received the _____."

3. List three tools of understanding illustrating the importance of contending in prayer:
   a. _____
   b. _____
   c. _____

Multiple Choice – Choose the best answer from the list below:

    A.   Embrace   C.   Blessing
    B.   Seek   D.   Receive

4. According to 2 Corinthians 5:7, God rewards those who diligently _____ Him.

5. You must learn to _____ God's love, grace and forgiveness before you can release it to others.

Continued on the next page.

True or False

6. We must focus our faith on the gift, not the Giver. _____

7. In every spiritual battle, we are to fight the good fight of faith. _____

8. Although patience is good, there are many shortcuts with God. _____

Scripture Memorization

9. Write out Psalm 95:7-8 and memorize it.

Lesson Twelve:
At the End of the Day

"You have taken account of my wanderings; put my tears in Your bottle. Are they not in Your book? Then my enemies will turn back in the day when I call; this I know, that God is for me."
Psalm 56:8-9

"Not that I have already obtained it or have already become perfect, but I press on so that I may lay hold of that for which also I was laid hold of by Christ Jesus. Brethren, I do not regard myself as having laid hold of it yet; but one thing I do: forgetting what lies behind and reaching forward to what lies ahead, I press on toward the goal for the prize of the upward call of God in Christ Jesus."
Philippians 3:12-14

"I have fought the good fight, I have finished the course, I have kept the faith."
2 Timothy 4:7

"Morning by morning he wakens me and opens my understanding to his will. The Sovereign Lord has spoken to me, and I have listened."
Isaiah 50:4-5 NLT

Have you ever attended a graduation ceremony? After working hard for years, the graduates have finally completed their journey. Tears flow from the family and friends gathered while at the same time, smiles of relief and joy are on the faces of the graduates. Together they realize that part of their lives is over. And yet, life is not over–it is just beginning! A grand adventure awaits as they put into practice everything they've learned.

And now, you're approaching the end of this class in your personal School of the Holy Spirit. Like graduation, this is not an end but rather the beginning of an exciting adventure into fresh applications of hearing God's vice today.

I. HAS GOD REALLY SAID?
God chooses each one of us to fulfill a distinct purpose and destiny in Him. The call of Jesus causes us to cast away the "fishing nets" of the things that are familiar to us to become pilgrims on a journey. Like Jesus' first disciples, we don't know what the future holds. Christ helps us to be determined, no matter what the cost is, to follow hard after Him in order to fulfill His will. Isn't that your desire?

We may struggle at times and even get frustrated, tempted to throw in the towel, but we continue. The once–bright pathway temporarily disappears. We thought we had heard our Master say where we were headed. Yet by sight, we may seemingly appear to be no further down the road than when we first began.

It is in these times that we must turn to our roadmap over and over again. We lean our ear in His direction to receive encouragement for today. Yes, it may be an arduous path, but it is an adventure. We must proceed. After all, these are the requirements: to hear God's voice and obey it!

A. The Enemy Attempts His Same Old Tricks
How often have we heard God speak clearly, only to have it followed by the devil's sly comeback, "Has God *really* said?"–which is the same question the serpent asked Eve in the Garden (see Genesis 3:1). The enemy has repeated those words in the ear of every person who has ever tried to follow the Lord God.

B. Undermining the Word of the Lord
Unless we have God's Word rooted deeply inside us, we can easily get off track because of Satan's insinuations. Vaguely trying to quote God's Word, we repeat Eve's mistake: "Don't eat–in fact, don't even touch it!" In fact, Eve added the last phrase about not touching it (see Genesis 3:3). Like Eve, we misquote God, and as a result, we are sometimes caught off balance.

II. RIGHT IN THE LINE OF FIRE
Sometimes we feel as though we are the direct target of spiritual warfare. It's because we are ambassadors of the One who has vanquished all the collective forces of the dark side. The devil lost his battle of coming against God Himself, so he shifted tactics and started going after those whom God loves.

A. Grace for the Battle
Like Jesus, our Messiah, in the Garden of Gethsemane, we must kneel before our Lord and Maker, and we receive grace and strength for the battle. Then we must put on the full armor of God and arm ourselves for the fight ahead (see Ephesians 6:11).

B. It's Time to Act on James 4:7
"Submit therefore to God. Resist the devil and he will flee from you."

1. Submit Everything to God
2. Resist the Devil–Take a Stand!
3. Watch as the Devil Runs Away from You!

III. TESTED BY THE WORD

"The words of the LORD are pure words; as silver tried in a furnace on the earth, refined seven times" (Psalm 12:6). Often, when we receive an exciting revelation from God, He uses the revelation itself to test us and purify us so that our character will be able to convey the word to others.

A. Four Examples of Those Who Were Refined by Fire
1. Abraham as recorded in Genesis 22
2. Joseph as recorded in Genesis 45
3. Moses as recorded in Exodus 32
4. David as recorded in 2 Samuel 15

B. God's Redemptive Purposes
Each of these men had received a promise, but when the testing of those words came, they each failed along the way. But God used their failures as part of their character-development process. Even our failures can be used to help keep God's word pure.

IV. WHAT IS YOUR RESPONSE?

If we hear God's voice and have been called to even a small task in building His Kingdom, let's rejoice that we have been found worthy to be called God's children and to be tested on the very promises He gives to us. But always remember the basics!

A. Lessons from 1 Corinthians 10:13
"No temptation has overtaken you but such as is common to man; and God is faithful, who will not allow you to be tempted beyond what you are able, but with the temptation will provide the way of escape also, so that you will be able to endure it."

B. Lessons from Romans 5:3-5
"And not only this, but we also exult in our tribulations, knowing that tribulation brings about perseverance; and perseverance, proven character; and proven character, hope; and hope does not disappoint, because the love of God has been poured out within our hearts through the Holy Spirit who was given to us."

God tests His very words on purpose so that we will reach our hand heavenward to grasp His hand of mercy and grace. He is a good Father. He wants us to grow up to be as much like His Son as we can be.

V. TESTIMONIES FROM MY PERSONAL JOURNEY

I can't spell out all the second-guessing I have been through, the sleepless nights, the wrestling against the demonic hosts, yes, the cost of moving forward, leaving one movement to cross over to the next. The cost of leaving family and friends to move to another geographic location just because God said so. Michal Ann and I picked up our cross many times to walk out God's words to us.

But we always knew we were in good company, following in the footsteps of others. Today, I have another price I pay. Right now, I walk alone. Yet even this is an opportunity to find hope in Christ, because there really is a silver lining that comes with every storm cloud.

It's worth the price–to hear His voice, to know His kiss, to sense His touch. Satisfaction does not come as much through finishing a task as it does through increased intimacy with Him. At the End of the Day, He is my journey's beginning–and its end. Yes, At the End of the day, I long to hear those words: *Well done, My faithful son. Well done!*

VI. THIS IS MY FATHER'S WORLD!

As I penned these words for this final lesson, my entire being was overwhelmed with the loveliness of God's presence. I had just come back in from my southern-facing front porch, which overlooked the beautiful hills of Franklin, Tennessee. The sun was setting, and the sky was ignited with a display of heavenly colors.

In gratitude to God, I lifted my glass and gave God a toast: "To the promises of God and to the God who promises!" With tears of gratitude, I then sang this old hymn to Him. So read these familiar words, and sing them if you know the tune:

> This is my Father's world,
> And to my listening ears
> All nature sings, and round me rings
> The music of the spheres.
> This is my Father's world:
> I rest me in the thought
> Of rocks and trees, of skies and seas;
> His hand the wonders wrought.
> This is my Father's world,
> The birds their carols raise,
> The morning light, the lily white,
> Declare their Maker's praise.
> This is my Father's world,
> He shines in all that's fair;

In the rustling grass I hear him pass;
He speaks to me everywhere.
This is my Father's world,
O let me ne'er forget
That though the wrong seems oft so strong,
God is the ruler yet.
This is my Father's world,
Why should my heart be sad?
The Lord is King; let the heavens ring!
God reigns; let the earth be glad![20]

VII. BECAUSE GOD IS GOOD — A PRAYER OF COMMITMENT

In the amazing name of Jesus, I declare that God is good all the time and that all things work together for good. I love the sound of Your voice, Lord; it brings such joy and comfort to me. Yes, I come to the garden alone, and the joy we share while we tarry there, none other has ever known. Give me more lessons in the School of the Spirit to better hear and discern Your voice. By grace, I make a commitment to obey Your Word and release the fragrance of Christ wherever I go. What an honor and privilege it is to hear Your voice today. Amen and Amen!

Do you hear Him speaking to you now? He's waiting to have a moment with you. Lean your head in a bit and you will hear more than words. You will hear the sound of love beating in His heart. He is your journey's end. At the End of the Day, knowing God is what hearing God is ultimately all about!

Reflection Questions
Lesson Twelve: At the End of the Day

Answers to these questions can be found in the back of the study guide.

Fill in the Blank

1. In a question as old as the Garden of Eden, everyone who has ever tried to follow the Lord God has heard these words: _____ _____ _____ _____?

2. Unless we have God's Word rooted deeply inside us, we can easily get off track because of Satan's _____.

3. List four examples of men in the Bible who were refined by fire:
   a. _____
   b. _____
   c. _____
   d. _____

Multiple Choice – Choose the best answer from the list below:

   A. Worthy   C. Faithful
   B. Gracious   D. Honored

4. If we hear God's voice and are called to do any task in His Kingdom, we rejoice because we have been found _____ to be called God's children.

5. 1 Corinthians 10:13 tells us that even when we endure temptation, that God is _____ to not allow us to be tempted more than we are able to endure without providing a way of escape.

Continued on the next page.

True or False

6. We are able to exult in our tribulations, knowing that they can produce many good things in our lives. _____

7. God tests us because He wants us to mature so we can grow up to be as much like His Son as we can be. _____

8. It is worth any price to hear His voice, to know His kiss, and to sense His touch. _____

Scripture Memorization

9. Write out Philippians 3:12-14 and memorize it.

Reflection Question Answers

Lesson One: As It Was in the Beginning
1. a. Talking to Him, b. Listening to Him when He talks to us.
2. Fellowship
3. Listen
4. B
5. D
6. True   7. False   8. False

Lesson Two: The Holy Spirit at Work Today
1. a. Guide you into all truth   b. Not speak on His own authority
   c. Speak what He hears (from God)   d. Tell you things to come.
2. Heart
3. Ghost
4. C
5. A
6. True   7. False   8. False

Lesson Three: The Sound of Many Rushing Waters
1. Verb, Proceed
2. Hear, Know, Obey
3. Any of the 20 "tools" listed in Section III.
4. Waters
5. Wilderness
6. False   7. True   8. True

Lesson Four: Walking in Our Kingdom Birthright
1. Possessions, Chosen
2. Priest, Prophet
3. Commands, Decrees, Desires, Orders
4. B
5. D
6. False   7. True   8. True

Lesson Five: Built Upon the Rock
1. Hearts
2. Logos, Rhema
3. Planning & Execution, Message & Vehicle, Whole & Part
4. Hear
5. Exercise
6. False   7. True   8. False

Lesson Six: Ten Practical, Personal Tools
1. Finger
2. Clean
3. Pride, Presumption, Missed Timing, Confusion
4. Speak
5. Counterfeit
6. True   7. False   8. True

Lesson Seven: Walking in Community
1. People
2. Whole
3. Unusual
4. Healing
5. Offended
6. True   7. False   8. True

Lesson Eight: Hearing with Discernment
1. Discerning of spirits
2. Detect
3. The Holy Spirit, the Human Soul, Demonic Evil Spirits
4. Agrees
5. Exalts
6. True   7. False   8. True

Lesson Nine: He Will Guide You!
1. Geiger counter
2. God's will is made known in the Word, God's will is confirmed through circumstances, The Holy Spirit speaks from where He dwells.
3. Conditions
4. Righteousness
5. Justice
6. False   7. False   8. True

Lesson Ten: Listening, Waiting and Watching
1. Listening, Waiting, Watching at the Gates
2. Disciple
3. Distraction
4. Watching
5. Vision
6. True   7. True   8. True

Lesson Eleven: Properly Responding to God's Voice
1. Responding
2. Blessing
3. It's Not Just for You, It Strengthens You in God, It Threatens the Enemy, It Takes a Team Working Together
4. Seek
5. Receive
6. False   7. True   8. False

Lesson Twelve: At the End of the Day
1. Has God Really Said?
2. Insinuations
3. Abraham, Joseph, Moses, David
4. Worthy
5. Faithful
6. True   7. True   8. True

End Notes

1. James W. Goll, *Hearing God's Voice Today* (Baker Books, 2016), p. 16.

2. Mark Virkler, quoted in Leonard LeSourd, ed., *Touching the Heart of God* (Old Tappan, NJ: Chosen Books, 1990), p. 59.

3. Dutch Sheets, quoted in Quin Sherrer, *Listen, God Is Speaking to You* (Ann Arbor, MI: Vine Books, 1999), p. 9.

4. Annie S. Hawks (1872); Author (refrain): Robert Lowry (1872), "I Need Thee Every Hour "

5. Quin Sherrer and Ruthanne Garlock, *The Beginner's Guide to Receiving the Holy Spirit* (Ann Arbor, MI: Vine Books, 2002), p. 45.

6. David Wilkerson, "What It Means to Walk in the Spirit," *Times Square Church Pulpit Series* (August 15, 1994), p. 4.

7. *Merriam-Webster's Collegiate Dictionary, 10th edition*, s.v. "tutor

8. Anne Morrow Lindbergh, *Gift From the Sea,* (New York: Pantheon Books, 2005), p. 94

9. James W. Goll, *The Beginner's Guide to Hearing God* (Ventura, CA: Regal Books, 2008), p. 137

10. James W. Goll, *The Coming Prophetic Revolution* (Grand Rapids, MI: Chosen Books, 2001), p. 125.

11. Quin Sherrer, Listen, *God Is Speaking to You* (Ann Arbor, MI: Vine Books, 1999), p. 26.

12. Jack Deere, *Surprised by the Power of the Spirit* (Grand Rapids, MI: Zondervan Publishing House, 1993), p. 212.

13. Michael Brown, *Revolution! The Call to Holy War* (Ventura, CA: Renew, 2000), pp. 57-58.

14. James W. Goll *The Lost Art of Practicing His Presence* (Shippensburg, PA: Destiny Image Publishing, 2005), p. 131

15. Richard Foster *Prayer: Finding the Heart's True Home* (San Francisco, CA: Harper, 1992) p. 146

16. The content of this lesson has been greatly inspired by, though not directly quoted from, the outstanding book *Is That Really You, God?* by Loren Cunningham. Loren Cunningham is the founder of Youth With A Mission. I would highly recommend this book to anyone desiring to learn more about hearing and discerning the voice of God. Used by permission.

17. James W. Goll, *Prophetic Foundations* (Franklin, TN: Ministry to the Nations, 2000), p. 35.

18. C. Peter Wagner, *Discover Your Spiritual Gifts* (Ventura, CA: Regal Books, 2005) p. 146

19. Sam Storms, *The Beginner's Guide to Spiritual Gifts* (Ann Arbor, MI: Vine Books, 2002), pp. 103-104.

20. Maltbie D. Babcock, "This Is My Father's World", words 1901, public domain.

About the Author

Dr. James W. Goll is the President of God Encounters Ministries, formerly known as Encounters Network, and has founded numerous ministries including Prayer Storm and Women on the Frontlines. He is a member of the Harvest International Ministries apostolic team and an instructor in the Wagner Leadership Institute and Christian Leadership University.

With great joy James has shared Jesus in more than 50 nations teaching and imparting the power of intercession, prophetic ministry, and life in the Spirit.

James is the prolific author of numerous books including *The Seer, The Lost Art of Intercession, The Coming Israel Awakening, Finding Hope,* and the award winning *The Lifestyle of a Prophet.* He has recorded multiple classes with corresponding study guides and full curriculum kits.

In the spirit of revival and reformation, James desires to facilitate unity in body of Christ by relationally networking with leaders of various denominational streams. His passion is to "win for the Lamb the rewards of His suffering." Praying for Israel is a burden of his heart, as Israel fulfills her role in the consummation of the ages.

James and Michal Ann were married for 32 years before her graduation to heaven in the fall of 2008. James has four adult children who are all married: Justin, GraceAnn, Tyler, and Rachel and a growing number of grandchildren. James makes his home in the rolling hills of Franklin, TN.

For More Information & Additional Resources:

James W. Goll
God Encounters Ministries
P.O. Box 1653
Franklin, TN 37065
Visit: www.GodEncounters.com or www.JamesGoll.com

Email: info@godencounters.com
Speaking Invitations: InviteJames@godencounters.com

Other Books by James W. and Michal Ann Goll

God Encounters
Prayer Storm
Intercession: The Power and Passion to Shape History
A Radical Faith
Women on the Frontlines Series
The Lost Art of Intercession
The Lost Art of Practicing His Presence
The Lost Art of Pure Worship
The Coming Israel Awakening
The Lifestyle of a Prophet
The Call of the Elijah Revolution
The Prophetic Intercessor
The Seer Expanded
Shifting Shadows of Supernatural Experiences
Empowered Prayer
Empowered Women
Dream Language
Angelic Encounters
Adventures in the Prophetic
Praying for Israel's Destiny
Living a Supernatural Life
Deliverance from Darkness
Exploring Your Dreams and Visions
God's Supernatural Power in You
The Reformer's Pledge
Prayer Changes Things
Passionate Pursuit: Getting to Know God and His Word
Finding Hope – Rediscovering Life after Tragedy
Releasing Spiritual Gifts Today
Hearing God's Voice Today

In addition, there are numerous study guides including: *Discovering the Seer in You, Exploring the Gift and Nature of Dreams, Prayer Storm, A Radical Faith, Deliverance from Darkness, Walking in the Supernatural Life, Finding Hope for Your Life* and many others with corresponding classes and curriculum kits.

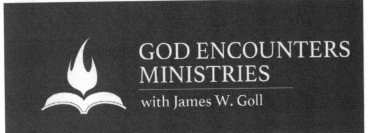

GOD ENCOUNTERS MINISTRIES
with James W. Goll

God Encounters Ministries started around twenty-five years ago in Missouri, originally called Ministry to the Nations. It was a natural - supernatural overflow of the relationship that James and Michal Ann Goll had with Jesus and each other. After moving to the Nashville, TN area in 1996, the ministry was renamed Encounters Network. Through the years the heart and core values of the ministry have remained exactly the same!

Now we are reaching more people than ever with the gospel of Jesus, teaching and imparting the power of prophetic ministry, intercession and life in the Spirit. We believe that God Encounters are for everyone! So visit our website and deepen your walk with God today!

For more info, visit: **GodEncounters.com**

Blog
Grow in your relationship with God. Enjoy poignant articles from James W. Goll that will inspire you.

Classes
18 Online Classes by James W. Goll. Great for self-study or to facilitate a small group in your home or church.

Media
Hundreds of FREE Audio and Video messages ready to revitalize you and give you hope! Access on demand.

Store
Cultivate revelation in your walk of faith. Dynamic resources to equip you and light your spiritual fire.

Made in the USA
San Bernardino, CA
01 February 2017